陝西歷史博物館
THE SHAANXI HISTORY MUSEUM

館藏精品鑒賞
APPRECIATION OF THE MUSEUM COLLECTION

楊培鈞　著
Yang Peijun

陝西人民教育出版社
SHAAXI PEOPLE'S EDUCATION PUBLISHING HOUSE

楊培鈞，1944 年生。1967 年於西北大學中文系畢業。曾長期從事文化文物業務管理工作。主持和參與組織過中華歷史名人諸葛亮、張騫、蔡倫等學術研究活動，擔任過第二屆和第三屆褒斜石門研究會會長。曾主編有《漢中地區名勝古迹》，發表過《論"漢魏石門十三品"》、《"漢三頌"價值論》、《旅游發展要重視歷史文化資源的開發利用》、《中華古文明的寶庫》等論文或文章多篇。現任陝西歷史博物館黨委副書記、副館長，陝西省博物館學會理事。

Mr Yang Peijun, born in 1944, graduated from the Chinese literature department of Northwest University in 1967. For quite a long time, He was engaged in the vocational work of the management of cultural and historical relics. He was in charge of or participated in the organization of the academic research exchanges for the Chinese famous historical personage Zhu Geliang, Zhang Qian and Cailun. And he was the chairman of the second and third seminar of the study of Shimen along the plank roadway near Bao and Xe gorge. Scenic spots and historical sites in Hanzhong region was his editorial work. He has published many essays and papers, such as On 13 Master Pieces Han and Wei Shimen (stone entrance), Value of the Three Eulogies of the Han period, the development of tourism should attach great importance to the expliotation of historical and cultural resourees and Tresure of Chinese ancient civilization. Mr Yang now is the deputy party secretary and deputy director of the Shaanxi History Museum. In addition to his position at the museum, he is also a member of Shaanxi, Museums society

卷首絮語

　　每當觀眾來到這里——陝西歷史博物館，那氣勢恢宏的建築、璀璨奪目的文物，曾使多少炎黃子孫、中外賓朋為之驚喜，為之振奮，為之怦然心動。從 1991 年 6 月 20 日起，她便以雄渾典雅的姿態，矗立于曾是十三朝帝都的西安，與大雁塔遙相呼應，向人們訴說着昨日的輝煌，展示着今日的風采，昭示着未來的希望。每天，成千上萬的游客絡繹不絕，把她視為周秦漢唐的藝術殿堂、中華文明的歷史長廊，在這里觀瞻徜徉，品評鑒賞，留下美好的記憶，帶走無盡的向往!

　　陝西歷史博物館現在收藏着各類文物 37 萬余件，尤以商周青銅器、唐代金銀器、歷代陶俑和唐墓壁畫獨領風騷，享譽中外。兩千多件青銅器中，有為數不少的國寶級珍品。900 余件金銀器，收藏之富名列全國之首。數以萬計的歷代陶俑千姿百態、風格迥异。400 余座唐墓出土的壁畫，總面積有 1000 平方米，獨步全國、在世界也絕無僅有。這些文物，是歷史對陝西的厚愛和饋贈，它記錄着中華民族在三秦大地繁衍生息的步履，傳遞着人類文明在神秘東方創造發展的信息。歷經人世的滄桑巨變，遭逢戰火的反復洗禮，目睹朝代的興衰更迭，它們幸存下來，又被集中起來，成為探求浩如烟海的古代典籍的形象佐證，成為解開撲朔迷離的歷史疑團的有力鎖鑰，成為認識紛繁宏富的文明發展的實物資料。它們不僅是中華民族的國之瑰寶，而且是世界人民的共同財富。

　　為了使廣大的中外游客更好地了解這些財富的真正價值，更深地領悟它們的文化內涵，我從已經展出的近 3000 件文物中，擷取出近百件精品，力求簡要而明晰地作以鑒賞，給觀眾深入的多角度的探求興趣提供一個基礎，希望它能為觀眾和文物之間架一座認識的橋梁。編選時，我把具有一定藝術性的歷史文物作為首選條件，目的是使觀眾得到美感享受和心靈的愉悅。這樣，就使那些雖然具有較高的歷史價值而缺乏藝術觀賞價值的文物只好暫時割愛，舍去未選。所選的每件文物，都以照片顯現原貌，幷力求將出土時間地點、大小尺寸、造型特點、藝術價值、歷史價值等叙述清楚，做到一文一圖，兩相對照，以便于披覽。由于水平所限，錯誤在所難免，敬祈讀者不吝指教。

楊培鈞

1994 年歲末

PREFACE

While the tourist entered the Shaanxi history museum, the perfect archi-
tecture and the splendid cultural relics let many descendant of Yan Huang and
the foreigners get great surprised and exercited with delightfuls. From 20th,
Jane in 1991, the museum standed in the ancient capital Xian,where 13 dynasties found the capitals with the splendid and elegant posture, which is in
echo with Dayan pogoda, and telling about the history of Xian and displaying
today's magnificance and showing the bright future. Everyday, thousands of
the tourists are in an endless stream, who regard it as the artistic hall of Zhou,
Qin, Han and Tang Dynasties, and the civilizational corridor of the chinese culture, who enjoy the gems and had very excellent time in appriation, also take
sweet memories.

Here collected 37000 pieces of relics, especially are famous for the collection of bronze wares of the Shang and Zhou Dynasties, gold and silver wares
of the Tang Dynasty, pottery figures and the frescoes of the tombs of the Tang
Dynasty, which gained great reputation. Among two thousands pieces of
bronze wares, many of them are gems of national class. Nine hundreds of gold
, silver wares is the first all over China. Thousands of the pottery figures are in
different style and shows the hundreds of postures. The fresco unearthed from
400 tombs of the Tang Dynasty, the total area is about 1000 m^2, which is the
unique all over the world. These gems, are the gift from the history, which are
the records of the development and people's life in Shaanxi, and information
of the eastern cultural splendour. Undergoing the changing of the dynasties
the baptism of the war, these relics were unearthed again, and suppied the
proof of the history and the mirror of the times, also gave us the key of researching the historical problems and ancient civilization. They are not only
the treasures of the chinese and also the richness of the people all over the
world.

In order to let the tourists know the real virtue of these treasures and understand the significance of them, we chosed about one hundred gems
among the exhibitioned 3000 pieces, supplying a simple and clear appriation
with deep angle and wide knowledge, and making a bridge between the relics
and the rivewers, which while our collecting and writting I choosed the pieces
with clear artistic features and special style, in order that the audience could
get the interest and happiness through appriating them. So some gems with
high historical virtue but lack of artistical virtue would not be collected in this
book. Every piece choosed in this book, we tried to show the size, the place
unearthed, the feature of style and the virtue of art and history through the
photos, we used one gem one picture which is easily for apprieciation. Because of the limited time and research level, the faulse might be in the
explaination please point it out, and thank you for your advise honestly.

Yang Peijun

1994

目　　錄

一、青銅器、銅器

二、金銀玉器

四、其它

Content

BRONLE WARE BRASS OR COPPER WARE

GOLDWARE SILVERWARE JADEWARE

EARTHENWARE & CHINAWARE

OTHER

陕西歷史博物館序言大廳
The Entrance Hall of Shaanxi History Museum

鳳柱斝（jiǎ）

商代晚期（公元前1200—前1028年）

通高41cm，口徑19.5cm，腹深16cm，重2.9公斤

1973年於陝西岐山縣賀家村西周墓出土

鳳柱斝侈口，口沿立雙柱，柱端各飾立體鳳鳥。腹分上下兩段，各飾雲雷紋饕餮面。腹面饕餮紋飾與補白雲雷紋平細不分，顯得文而不猙。器底較平，略向外鼓，腹側有犀首鋬，鋬面爲竊曲紋。下有三棱錐足，尖端外撇。

鳳柱斝雙柱端的立體鳳鳥別具一格，十分罕見。鳳鳥高冠豎起，長羽飄舉，圓目鼓睜，體飾花羽短翎，鳥尾平伸。雙柱巧妙地用作鳥足，鳳鳥恰似佇足舉目遠眺。鳳鳥造型身姿矯健，體軀華貴，生機勃勃，活力盎然。

鳳鳥在古代是一種吉祥的象徵。東漢許慎在《說文解字》中這樣解釋："鳳，神鳥也，出于東方君子之國，翱翔四海之外……見則天下大安寧。"鳳鳥用來裝飾雙柱，使斝器引人入勝，惹人喜愛。

斝是一種溫酒器。鳳柱斝是賀家村西周墓出土的35件青銅器中最爲精美的一件。

Jia，a Wine Vessel with a Mouth of Double-phoenix-pillar Relief

The Late Shang Dynasty (B. C1240—1028)

H. 41cm，D. of mouth 19.5cm，Depth. 16cm，W 2.9kg.

Unearthed in 1973 at Hejia-cun of Qishan County, Shaanxi, from one mausoleum.

It has wide mouth, at the edge standing double pillars, on the top are the phoenix. The body was devided two parts, decorated by cloub reins and tao Die masks. The Tao Die design with the cloud veins are very fine, show perfect but not fierce. The bottom is flat, and a little bit raised outside, at the flank there are Hino Head Ban, the Ban decorated with Qie Qu veins. There are three pyramid feet, the tip are leaving cat.

The double phoenix fly their own colours and is seldom seen. The phoenix lift the high crown, with smug leather. Glaring the round eyes, the body decorated the short feather, the tail extend silently. And the pillars just are the birds feet ingeniously, the birds just stand still and look into the distance from the high Jia. The shape of the phoenix is strong and vigorous and show the luxurious and energatic.

Phoenix is the signify of good fortune in the ancient times. Xu shen of East Han Dynasty explained in his book "Explaining the word" like this, "the phoenix a kind of fairy bird, born from the East of the noble land, hovering all over the world…Of you see it, the country will be full of love and peace". Decorated the Jia with the phoenix and let it be fascinating.

Jia is a kind of wine vessel. This piece is the best one of the 35 pieces bronzes which were unearthed from West Zhou mausoleum of He jia-cun.

鳳柱斝

Jia, a Wine Vessel with a Mouth of
Double-phoenix-pillar Relief

四足鬲

晚商（公元前 13—前 11 世紀）

通高 23.2cm，口徑 21cm，腹深 16.1cm，重 4.8 公斤

1981 年於陝西城固縣龍頭村窖藏出土。

此鬲寬沿外折，子母口，矮頸，飾一圈雷紋；四足中空，組成鬲腹。腹身飾四個獸面紋。獸面大眼珠如圓球，浮雕突出，炯炯有神；額頂有夸張的耳，鼻嘴向下，腹體填滿雲雷紋。刻紋寬深勻稱，內填黑色固體。整個造型深厚凝重，紋飾富麗。綫條剛勁有力，講究對稱。一般鬲只有三足，此鬲為四足，目前在全國獨一無二。

這只鬲具有明顯的地域性特征。它的出土地城固縣在漢中地區，殷商時是巴的方國。巴人作為一個民族，英武頑強，一度曾控制過漢水中上游。周武王伐紂時，曾得到巴人的支持和參與，戰勝殷商后，受到周族宗室的分封，成為"巴方"。巴人進入漢中遠遠早于商人。從城固縣滑水河沿岸的蘇村、五郎、蓮花、龍頭等地先后出土的 486 件青銅器來看，絕大部分是用于戰爭的兵器及其附件，又多為窖藏。既反映出它們與殷商的文化聯系，又反映出它們和周族的密切關系，還保持着自己獨有的特點。它們以自己的聰明才智，創造出了獨具風格的青銅文化，成為中華民族古代文化的一個組成部分。

鬲是烹飪器，流行于商周時期。戰國晚期青銅鬲從祭器和生活用具中消失。與這只四足鬲在同一地點先后出土的共有 13 種 75 件青銅器。可能為逃避殷人征討埋藏起來，以備后用的。

Li, a Cooking Vessel with Four Legs

The Late Shang Dynasty (13th—11th century B. C)

H 23.2cm, D. of mouth 21cm. Depth. 16.1cm, W. 4.8kg.

Unearthed in 1981 from the cellar at Long-tou-cun of Cheng-gu County, Shaanxi.

It is wide edge and fold out, eighttwi-mouth, short neck, decorated with round thunder designs. Inside the four legs, are empty, which formes the stomach of this vessel. There are four animal-face designs on it. The eye of the animal like the ball, relief very well, bright and shining; there are overstate ears on the forehead, mouths and noses are down ward; it was carvedfull of cloud and thunder (yun and leiveins) veins. The designs are wide and deep and well balanced, filled with black solid in them. The whole shape is simple and vigorous, with magnificent veins decorations. The lions are bold and graceful, which is particular about symmetry. Generally. Li has three legs, but this one has four legs. At present, it is the only one in China. It has obvious features of regional. Chenggu county where it is unearthed located Hanzhong area, at Shang Dynasty, here is Ba Kindom. Being one race, the people of Ba were brave, who once controled the upper and middle reaches of Hanshui River. When Zhou Dynasty, Zhou Wu Wang (king Zhou Wu) sent armed forces to supperss Zhou Wang, who got the help from people at Ba, after they defeated the Shang, they gained the nobility from Zhou Clan, so called "Ba Tang". People of Ba entered Han Zhong more earlier than Shang people. Allow 486 pieces unearthed bronzes from Sucun, Wulang, Lianhua, Long tou by the Xushui river at Chenggu County, we found that most of them are weapons or accessories, and mostly were hiden in the cellar. It reflected that they connected with the culture of Shang and they had good realation with the Zhou Clan, but they still kept their own unique feature. They created the unique bronze culture.

Li, a kind of cooking utensil, was popular in Shang and Zhou dynasties. As a sacrifioal object and a vessel for everyday life, bronze li disappeared in the late period of Warring States Period. 75 bronze wares in 13 types were found at the same site with the four-legged. They might be hidden by Ba people in order to escape from The Yin Shang's controling and wanted to use later.

四足鬲
Li, a Cooking Vessel with Four Legs

圓鼎

西周早期

通高 40.2cm，口徑 32cm，重 11.65 公斤

1981 年 4 月於陝西寶雞市紙坊頭墓葬出土

鼎口略呈圓三角形，方唇，平折沿，上有方立耳，略外侈，腹略呈垂腹狀，器較淺，底平闊，三足頗長，形為束腰蹄足。鼎蓋薄板扁平，蓋面正中有立耳提紐，周圍飾有三個倒立的夔龍，可倒置成三足淺盤。

圓鼎造型比例適當，穩重華美。蓋面飾六組饕餮紋。腹上部飾一周饕餮紋帶，共六組，每組中央飾一短扉棱。腹下部飾一周蕉葉紋，共十三組，蕉葉內裝飾對稱的豎立夔龍紋，每葉一對，頭向上，尾相接。都以雲雷紋襯地。鼎足上端飾獸面紋，并有突出的短扉棱。器表夔龍紋如浮雕突起，綫條粗獷有力，有不同於西周典型青銅器的地域性風格。

圓鼎是西周時強國國君的器物。強國為分封在西北地區的一個小諸侯國。

Tripod

The early stage of Weatern Zhou Dynasty.

H. 40.2cm, D. of mouth 32cm, W. 11.65kg.

Excavated at Zhifang tou, Baoji city in April 1981

The shape of mouth is round-triangle slightly, square lip, flat edge three columnar legs. The tripod is hanging down in shape, it is shallower, the bottom is wide and flat. Three legs are rather long and splender waist and hoots feet in shape. The lid is thin and flat there is a squar lug in the center of it, around which are three cabic ridgy knobs, which can be a plate after-turned over to stand as three legs.

The proportion of the tripod is suitable in shaped, it is steady and splendid. Decorated with Tao Tie design on the lid. On the neck of the tripod, is engraved the Tao Die designs, altogether six pairs there is one short ridge between each pair, which on the wall there are decorated two symmetrical plantain leaf designs composed of vertical ogre-dragon patterns. There is one pair of each leaf, heads are up and tails linked. Designed with cloud and thunder vein. The columnar legs are bulging out and decorated with animal mask designs, there are ridges engraved. The ogre-dragon engraved like relief, the lines are vigorous and graceful, it has the unique district feature which is different from the trpical bronze of Western Zhou Dynasty. This tripod is a utensil of the King who control the Kingdom Yu, which was a very small duck kingdom in the northwest under the Zhou emperor.

圓 鼎
Tripod

龍紋大鼎

西周早期

通高122cm，口徑83cm，重226公斤

1979年於陝西淳化縣史家原村出土

大鼎沿外折，沿上雙耳對稱聳立，上端略呈外侈。鼎腹呈垂腹狀，深腹，腹底平闊。鼎腹中部加飾三環狀耳，環耳作立獸形。三足呈柱足形，上粗中細，下轉蹄形。

鼎腹上部飾一圈龍紋帶，龍首居中，左右兩條龍身，為單首雙體龍紋。龍首突起，雙目突出，中央為一短扉棱。龍身蜿蜒伸展，龍尾卷起，全身飾陰刻勾連雲紋，背有鰭，獨角，角上有傘形冠蓋，身下一足四爪。粗大雙耳外部，飾有兩兩相對龍紋，獨角雙足，尾部卷曲。鼎上面飾獸面紋和短扉棱。全鼎共有五耳，為青銅鼎所僅見。

這是一件形體龐大、深厚凝重的青銅重器。形體氣勢磅礴，裝飾簡練明快，風格樸實，不失華美，在圓形鼎中別具一格。其造型基本保持了殷商晚期胎壁厚實、形體恢宏、凝重莊嚴的風格。它是目前存世最大的一件西周時期的青銅器。

"鼎"在我國夏商周三代，均被視為"傳國寶器"，周武王伐紂滅商獲得寶鼎，其子周成王把九鼎運回都城鎬京，舉行了隆重的定鼎儀式，從此，九鼎就成為王權的象征。鼎上以龍紋作裝飾，是為了標榜自己是龍屬龍子，也是王權思想的一種反映。

Tripod with Dragon Designs

The early stage of western Zhou Dynasty

Excavated at Shijiayuan, Chunhua County. in 1979

H. 122cm，D. of mouth 83cm，W. 226kg.

The edge of the tripod are bulging out，there are two symmetrical ears which extend out on upper. The wall is vertical and the stomach is deep，with flat bottom，decorated with three ring-shaped ears on the abdomen，the ring-shaped ear is standing animal in shape. Three legs like three pillars，upper is strong，middle part little indented under is hoof in shape.

On the neck of the tripod，decorated with a dragon design，the head is in the center，left and right are the dragons，which is one head with two strong body. The head is projecting round eyes，there is a short arris in the center. The dragon is wrigging，the tails are rolling up，engraved with designs in intaglio，there is dorsal fin and one horn which has the umbrella-shaped crown，also a foot with four claws. Decorated with double dragon designs around the wide ears，which has one horn and two feet，the tail is rolling. Engraved with animal mask designs on the upper legs and there are short arrises too. There are five ears altogether，it is the unique feature all of the tripods.

This is one heavy bronze which is strong shape and simple and bright with luxry style and is of unique pattern among the round tripods. It kept the style of Late Shang Dynasty Which has the thick wall，strong shape and dignified manner. And it is the largest bronze tripod at the Western Zhou Dynasty excavated in China.

"Ding" (tripod) was regarded as the "Holly Utensil of the Land" at Xia，Shang and Zhou Dynasty，Zhou King Wuwang got the holly tripod after he destoryed Shang Zhou，his son Zhou Chengwang transported the tripod to the capital—Hao Jing (in Xi'an)，then made a great ceremony of laiding the tripod. From then on，the tripod became the symbol of imperial power. Dragon is worshiped by the chinese people，for this reason，dragon designs on the tripod means that the makers are desendents of the dragon，and it is also a mirror of imperial powerful thoughts.

龍紋大鼎
Tripod with Dragon Designs

折方彝

西周·昭王時期（公元前1004—前986年）

通高 40.7cm，口縱橫19.2×24cm，腹深19.2cm，重12.8公斤

1976年12月於陝西扶風縣莊白一號窖藏出土

彝蓋呈廡殿式屋頂，蓋紐呈硬山屋頂形狀，正脊兩端懸出，四角及中綫有鏤空棱脊，蓋頂蓋紐均飾倒置饕餮紋。彝腹壁呈圓弧狀鼓出，上飾饕餮紋，鼻準綫及四面有八條棱脊。圈足與彝體有明顯分界，器沿及圈足飾瀕尾夔紋。通體用繁密的細雷紋襯地。

折方彝造型雄偉，紋飾繁褥，浮雕峻銳。饕餮是古代傳說中的一種有首無身的貪婪怪獸，這裏被刻畫得獰獰怪異，使整個器物給人以莊重神秘、令人敬畏之感。器蓋對銘，蓋內各鑄40字，大意為：王在某地賞賜給一個叫"折"的人青銅和奴隸，折便為父乙鑄了這件彝器以誌紀念。

方彝是一種方形的盛酒器具。方彝在商代即已出現，到西周中晚期絕迹。

The Zhe's Square Wine Vessel（Zhe Fang Yi）

During the reign of king Zhao of the Western Zhou Dynasty.

Excavated at pit No. 1, Zhuangbaicun, Fufeng County, Shaanxi, in December 1976.

Its cover looks like a roof of a palace; its central knob like the hip and gable roof; the right arrises are suspending; on its four corners and the central line are perforated ridge-typed arrises; the cover and the knob are adorned with resersed "taodie" (monstrous animal) designs. The wall with bigger taodie designs. The wall of abdomen is arc-shaped extending out, with taodie designs, there are eight arrises on the central lines and four sides. And a clear decoration between the ring foot and the bulk, around the rim of the vessel and its ring foot and the bulk, are ogre-

dragon designs with tails coiled up. Decorated with very fine thunder vein on it.

The shape is grand and magnificent, designs are over-laborate, relief is vigorous. Taodie is a kind of monstrous animal which was very greedy without body, just a head in the ancient fairy folks. Here is a kind of monstrous carved very strange and ferocious, let the vessel show grave and mysterious, we would hold in awe and veneration while we see it.

There are inscriptions both on the vessel and cover, each having 40 characters, to the effect that King Zhao rewarded Zhe some bronze ware and a number of slaves, so Zhe cast this vessel for his father Yi.

"Fang Yi" is a kind of square wine vessel. It had appeared in Shang Dynasty and disappeared in Mid and Late Western Zhou Dynasty.

折方彝
The Zhe's Square Wine Vessel

象尊

西周中期·穆王時期（公元前985—前931年）

通高21cm，長38cm，腹深13.8cm，重3.5公斤

1975年於陝西寶鷄市茹家莊西周墓出土

象鼻作流，彎卷上舉，鼻端前后分叉，前叉呈凹槽，后叉呈坡型。象牙伸出隨鼻彎曲。兩耳豎起，微向前傾。雙目圓凸注視前方。象背呈圓弧形，腹腔中空，背上有蓋。蓋裝有雙環鈕，蓋上和器體還有兩個小半環，系一"8"形鏈，可啟閉而不脫落。短尾呈弧綫下垂，四足粗壯短小。

整個器體輪廓酷似野猪，體態渾圓概括，四肢穩定如柱，造型笨拙憨樸，給人變形美感。后臀和前胛節有鳳鳥組成的團花紋，其間填以雷紋，并以細雲紋襯地。

這件象尊出土時，還同時出土陶器、青銅器和玉石器等1500余件。墓主是西周穆王時期的強伯，其身份相當于大夫。強伯和正妻分葬于兩個墓室，強伯之妾隨強伯同穴殉葬。兩墓中還有九具被殺殉的奴隸骨架。據專家認為："西周考古發掘中，這種同穴妾殉葬的現象還是第一次發現。"象尊原陪葬在強伯惇室内。

象尊是一種青銅禮器，屬獸類尊。青銅器里，一般通稱走獸形的容酒器為獸尊，按其具體形狀，又可分為牛尊、象尊、羊尊、鳥型尊等。

The Elephant-shaped Wine Vessel (elephant-ahaped Zun)

In the time of king mu of Western Zhou Dynasty（B. C985－B. C931）

H. 21cm, L. 38cm, Depth 13.8cm, W. 3.5kg.

Excavated in the Rujia village, Baoji city, Shaanxi in 1975.

The trunk is the flow pipe, which rolled and raised high, and the top separated two parts. The front is a hollow trough in shape, and the back is slope is shape. Tusks exposed by the trunk, and the ears pricked up and eyes goggling. The back is in shape ofan arc, the belly is empty inside, there a cover on the back, There is a double-ring knob on teh cover, there are two small half-ring which xonnwxted, with a "8" -shaped chain. The cover could open and would not fall down. Short tail is dangling and four legs are short but strong.

The whole shape looks like wild boar, the body is round and fat, four lets are steady as columnars; the model is simple and honest, ebhabcing our impressing of its being out of shape. Engraved the designs of phoenix on the back buttock and front shoulder, also decorated with fine thunder veins.

When it was excavated, found some potteries, bronze, jade and stone utensils altogether 1500 pieces, the master of the tomb was Duck Yu in the time of King Mu of Western Zhou Dynasty, whose status was Dafu, Duck Yu and his wife were buried in two tombs seperately, and his concubine followed him burial together. There are nine slaver's skeletons who were killed as burited for their master. The expert considered "This is the first time that the concubine buried alive in the same tomb in engaging and excavating in archaeology stuies about Western Zhou Dynasty. "Xiang Zun"was buried in the Duke Yu's tomb.

The ware is a kind of bronze sacrificial vessele, beloning to the animal class vessels. In the bronze wares, generaly, called the animal-shaped vessel as animal zun. Allow the model, it could be divided as ox-shaped, elphant-shaped, goat shaped, and bird-shaped and so on.

象尊
The Elephant-shaped Wine Vessel

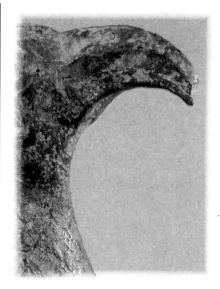

三足鳥尊

西周中期·穆王時期（公元前985年—前931年）

通高23cm，長30cm，腹深10.6cm，重3公斤

1975年4月於陝西寶鷄市茹家莊西周墓出土

鳥喙彎長，鳥首微昂，體態豐滿，體腔中空，背開方口，口上有蓋。遍飾羽紋，尾部寬垂，寬尾兩邊下垂地方飾花翎紋。三足粗短，上飾鱗紋。

整個造型趨于寫實，神態昂揚，充滿活力，給人穩定自信、任重道遠的感受。工匠又能從器物實際出發，大膽增加一足，構成三角形，使鳥器穩而不撲。另據中國古代神話傳說，西王母有三足鳥，是替西王母取食的青鳥。從此鳥造型上看，也有可能取其傳說之義。

三足鳥尊出土自強伯椁室中。當時，三足鳥尊共出土兩件，其形制和大小一樣。同椁室還出土有各類青銅器物和陶器等67件。

The Bird-shaped Wine Vessel with Three Legs

In the Time of King Mu of Western Zhou Dynasty（985 —931B. C）

H. 23cm, L. 30cm, Depth. 10.6cm, W. 3kg.

Excavated at Rujia village, Baoji city, Shaanxi in April 1975.

The beak is long and bend, the head hold up slightly. The shape is chubby, the belly is empty inside, there is a square mouth with a lid on the back. Engraved leather veins, tail is wide and Engling, at the two sides of the wide tail, designed the leather veins. Three legs are strong and short with the scale veins.

The whole shape is tending to real, the manner is high-spirited and full of energy, shows the steady, self-confidence and that the task is heavy and the road ahead is long. The craftsman could designed allow the fact, added one leg by his bold, which formed a triangle shape and let the vessel be steady. Also from the Chinese ancient fairy folk, it was said that the mother of West King had a bird with three legs, and the bird was a green bird which took food for her. From the shape, we know that it might be designed by the story.

This vessel excavated in the tomb of Duke Yu. At that time, like this vessel, we got another one, same design and same size. We excavated 67 pieces of bronze wares and pottery wares from the same tomb.

三足鳥尊
The Bird—shaped Wine Vessel with Three Legs

獏(mò) 尊

西周中期•穆王時期（公元前985年—前931年）

通高20.1cm，長34cm，腹深10cm，重3.16公斤

1975年4月於陝西寶雞市茹家莊西周墓出土

獏首一付大圓耳，一對雙環目，額頂飾一棱形。長嘴突出，前端微凹作流，后部尾巴作鋬。體軀肥厚，四腿粗短，背上開口，口上有蓋。蓋鈕鑄一立虎，蓋後和器身鑄有小環，"8"形鏈使器蓋相連，可以啟閉，不相脫離。後臀和前胛飾有變體鳳鳥組成的團花紋，蓋內鑄有八字銘文："弜伯匈井姬用盂錐。"

獏是一種熱帶哺乳動物，皮厚毛少，前肢四趾，后肢三趾。獏尊造型生動自然，圓耳雙目作警惕狀，似正在駐足側耳聆聽，又似在注目觀察動靜。蓋鈕立虎也似側耳駐足。虎尾下拖，作覓食欲撲之狀。

獏尊是弜伯正妻井姬墓內陪葬品，同墓出土各類青銅器23件。除一件雙環段為"弜伯自作用器"外，其余均為弜伯為井姬所作的器物。

Tapir-shaped Wine Vessel

In the time of King of Nu of Western Zhou Dynasty（B. C 985－931）

H．20.1cm，L．34cm，Depth．10cm，W．316kg.

Excavated at Rujia Village，Baoji city，Shaanxi in April 1975.

On the head of the tapir, there are a pair of big ears, a pair of doublering jecting, the front part is a bit hollow as the flow, the back park tail is the handle. The body chubby, four legs short and strong with an opener on the back and a lid. The knob on the lid is a strong tiger, there are small rings on the back of lid and vessel chained with "8" — shaped chain, then could open the lid and not fall down. engraved the designs of phoenix on the buttock and front shouder. Inside the lid are inscribed with 8 characters to the effect that Yu Bu made this vessel for his wife Jing ji. Tapir is a kind of mammal lives in the tropical area. Thick skin and less fur. Front limb has four toes, and the back limb has three toes. MoZun is vivid in shape, round ears and double eyes are in the mood of sharp vigilace, looks like listen to something and watching out for the movemment. The standing tiger on the lid, also stands still, the tail dangling down, which want to spring after finding the food.

"Mo Zun" was the burried vessels in the tomb of Yu Bo's wife whose name was Jingji, from the same tomb, excavated 23 pieces bronze wares. Besides one bouble-ring Yin with the words "use for Yu Bo", the left ones were the vessels which Yu Bo made for his wife Jingji.

獏尊
Tapir-shaped Wine Vessel

史牆盤

西周共王時期（公元前930—前916年）

通高16.2cm，口徑47.3cm，深8.6cm，重12.5公斤

1976年12月於陝西扶風縣莊白村窖藏出土，同時出土的還有瘣鐘等103件青銅器

盤敞□，淺腹，圈足，腹外附雙耳。

此盤鑄造精致，紋飾優美。腹表飾垂冠分尾鳳鳥紋，圈足飾兩端上下卷曲的雲紋，并以回旋綫條組成的雲雷紋填地。

盤是商周時期祭祀燕享中常見的盛器。此盤內底部有銘文18行，284字，是建國后發現的銅器銘文最長的一篇。銘文記述了周王朝先王和當朝天子的豐功偉績，自敘了微氏家族事奉周王朝的家世。微氏家族世代為周王室的史官，牆為了贊揚其先祖功德，祈求多福，作器以為紀念。

史牆盤是研究西周歷史、政治制度、社會經濟等的珍貴史料。文字通篇用韵，文氣貫通。結體凝煉，波磔圓潤，字迹雋麗，書法精湛。

此盤銘文光鮮如新，對考察金文書法極為有利。從書寫角度看，是真實精美的篆引筆法，在西周作品中極為少見。史牆盤與虢季子白盤、散氏盤的銘文書法，在西周金文大篆中位置顯赫，都是罕見的精品。

Historic Ggrapher Qiang's Plate

In the time of King Gong of Western Zhou Dynasty

H. 16.2cm, D. of mouth 47.3cm, Depth. 8.6cm W. 12.5kg.

It was unearthed in pit No, 1 at Zhuangbaicun in Fufeng County in December 1976, while excavated Bronze Bell altogether 103 pieces bronzes.

Plate is the oridinary vessels which was using for sacrifices in Shang and Zhou Dynasty.

This is the plate which is uncovered, had a round belly, a ring foot and two side ears.

It was casted delicately, with magnificent decorations. on the part of the belly wall are designs of phoenix with droping topknots and separated tails; while on the ring foot, it is dorned with ragged curve veins, helping with fine circle lines as the cloudy and thurder veins. On the bottom inside the plate, there is an inscription of 18 lines with 284 characters, which is the largest inscription of bronze after liberation the insprition traces the heroic exploits of the kings in early Zhou Dynasty and at present it also has brief account which tells the development of Wei's family who served for Zhou Dynasty. Wei's family were the historical officers of King of Western Zhou Dynasty, Qiang made this plate as memory in order to praise the virtues of his ancestors and pray for good fortune.

This plate is precious historical data for researcging the history, political system, society ecomomic of Western Zhou Dynasty. This artical used rhyme, which was written in an easy and fluent style. The calligraphy of the inscription is perfect, which is concise, mellow and full. The words are bright as new, it's helpful for inscription Jin character. From the writing way, we found that it is real Zhuan Style, which is seldom seen in the articales of Western Zhou Dynasty. The calligcaphy of Qiang plate, Guo Jizi white plate and San, plate the illustrious status in Jin characters of Western Zhou Dynasty, they are gems which are seldom seen.

史墙盤
Historic Grapher Qiang's Plate

史墙盤銘文拓片
Carved Inscription of Historic Ggrapher Qiang's Plate

冬簋 (duēng guǐ)

西周·穆王時期（公元前985年—前931年）

通高21cm，口徑22cm，腹深12.5cm，重5公斤

1975年於陝西扶風縣莊白村墓葬出土

此簋侈口，帶蓋。蓋與器表均飾鳳鳥紋。四對垂冠鳳鳥，兩兩相對，填以雷紋。雙耳作立體鳳鳥，昂首豎冠，挺脯斂翅，鳥足作垂珥。造型樸實端莊，紋飾高雅華美，雙耳匠心獨運。

蓋內和器底各鑄銘文134字，記載了一次戰役的經過。內容記述某年六月，伯冬率師抗擊淮戎，斬獲百人首級，繳獲武器135件，奪回俘虜114人。伯冬感念亡母的福德，作了這件器物。

冬簋器身鳳鳥作對稱回顧形排列，鳥冠華麗，鳥尾逶迤，線條粗獷簡明。這種大鳳紋為西周中期最為流行的具有特徵性的紋飾。它蓋器同銘，篆書行款一致，為一人手筆。筆意含蓄，不怒自威，器銘顯得清秀，蓋銘顯得厚重，是一件具有高度藝術水平和歷史價值的佳作。

簋是商周時期用於盛稻粱黍稷的食器。西周時，簋與鼎作為重要的禮器，有一套完整的用鼎制度。據文獻記載，天子用九鼎八簋，諸侯七鼎六簋，大夫五鼎四簋，元士三鼎二簋。

Dong Gui Food Container

In the time King Mu of the Western Zhou Dynasty (985 −931B. C)

H. 21cm, D. of mouth 22cm. Depth of belly 12.5cm. W. 5kg.

Unearthed in one of the tombs of the Western Zhou Dynasty, Zhuangbaicun, Fu feng County, Shaanxi in 1975.

The chacacter "Gui" denotes vessells which hold various kinds of food.

This piece, with a flared mouth, a cover, and two ears. It is adrones both on the parts of the cover and the ware itself with designs of phoenix. Four pairs of phoenix with drooping top-knots on the two sides facing each other symmertrically; with cloud and thunder designs to fill the blank as a foil, and on the parts of two ears with two phoenixes standing chins up dangling earring.

The shape is simple and dignified, the designs are elegant and perfect, two ears designed out of special insight.

There are inscription both on the cover and the vessel itself each having 134 chacacters recording the resitant warefare. It says that June in one year, Bo Dong and his troops against Huai Rong, in the war, seized 135 pieces of weapons, including lances and sheilds and 114 men who fell into the enemy's hands.

Bo Dong consider that this was owing to the blessing of his deceased mother, so he made this vessel.

There are inscription to the same effect both on the cover and the vessel. Zhuan Character was written by one people. The calligraphy is magnificent, the one on the vessel shoes delivate and pretty, the one on the cover is dignified. It is a superb masterpiece with high class of arts and historical value.

Gui is a kind of food container which was popular in the Shang and Zhou Dynasty. In the Western Zhou Dynasty, Gui and Tripod "Ding" were very important sacrifial vessels, and there was a complete system of using tripod. From the historical documents say that, the Kings used nine tripods and eight Guis, Dukes used seven tripods and six Guis, Dafu—five tripods and four Guis. Yuanshi—three tripods and two Guis.

戜簋
Dong Gui Food Container

戜簋銘文拓片
Carved Inscription of Dong Gui Food Container

儆匜（ying yi）

西周中期

通高 20.5cm，腹寬 17.5cm，長31.5cm，重3.85公斤

1975年2月於陝西岐山縣董家村出土

匜□平直前伸，腹鼓圓，四只羊足，尾部為獸形鋬環。

匜身帶一平蓋，蓋前為虎首，覆于流□，□治下節一道竊曲紋和凸弦紋。器蓋與腹底有157字銘文，是一篇完整的訴訟判決詞。

銘文記述了有一年三月末，周王與伯揚父在上宮定下判決詞。內容為懲罰牧牛違約誣告行為。牧牛是儆的下屬，分管放牛的奴隸。按律應打一千鞭，受墨刑，并以黑巾蒙頭。后大赦為打五百鞭，罰銅三百鍰（huán，一鍰等于六兩）。儆用得到的銅鑄了這件匜，以作紀念。

這篇銘文是我國目前發現最早的一篇法律判決書，是研究我國法律史的重要史料。

匜也是古代洗手時盛水的用具。古人洗手是把匜里的水倒在手上，下邊用盤承接，與后來把手浸在水盆里的洗法不同。

Ying Yi（water vessel）

The Mid-Western Zhou Dynasty

H. 20.5cm, W. 17.5cm, L. 31.5cm. Weight. 3.85kg.

Excavated at Dong jia cun, Qishan County, Shaanxi in Feb. 1975.

The flat is extending forward, belly is round, with four sheep feet. There is an sanimal-shaped handle-ring. It has a lid a tiger head in front of it, which covers the flowing-mouth, undered the edge of it, adorned with ragged curve designs and raised floral designs and raised designs. There is an inscription of 157 characters inside the lid and the vessel, which is a complete court verdict.

The inscription says that at the end of may one year, the King and BoYangfu ordered the verdict. The details is about punishment on account of MuNiu who broke a contract and made a trumped-up case. MuNiu was Yi's subordinate who sepenised the slavers of heading cattle. Allow the low, he should be whipped one thousand and covered the head with a black cloth. Later he got the general ardon then was whipped five hundred. And a penalty of copper 300 Huan（1Huan = 6Liang）Ying casted this vessel Yi with the copper as a mark.

This inscription is the earliest verdict of excavated up to now which is the important historical virtue of researching the history of chinese law.

Yi is a vessel of holding water for washing hands. In ancient times, the people pured water from Yi on the hands, under with a plate receiving the dirty water. It's quite different from washing hands in a basin later.

儶匜
Ying Yi

儶匜銘文拓片銘文之一
Carved Inscription of YingYi
Inscription One

儶匜銘文拓片銘文之二
Carved Inscription of YingYi
Inscription Two

牛尊

西周中期（公元前1027—
前771年）

通高24cm，身長38cm

1967年於陝西岐山縣賀家
村出土

牛頭平伸向前，雙目圓睜突出，雙角圓弧后伸，兩耳左右平伸。軀體壯碩渾圓，牛尾緊縮臀后。四腿圓柱短足，挺直有力。造型簡練寫實，構圖概括夸張。器身以雲紋和夔龍紋裝飾，紋飾豪放，綫條粗闊。作者巧妙地利用牛的各個部位，以牛身爲器，牛蹄爲足，引牛舌爲流，盤牛尾作柄，牛背開蓋注酒，蓋鈕虎形，溶實用性和藝術性爲一體，給人憨厚馴良的撲拙美感，而大塊面舒朗的裝飾風格，則給人華美的藝術感染。

專家認爲：在古代，舉行"裸祭"儀式都需特製的器物，牛尊就是祭祀專用的酒具。

Ox-shape Zun (wine vessel)

The Mid-western Zhou Dynasty (1027－771).

H. 24cm, L. 38cm.

Unearthed at Hejiacun, Qishan County, Shaanxi in 1967.

Ox head is extending forward, two eyes goggling, double horns are exlending back-ward, two eyes streching to right and left the body strong and chubby, the tail closed the bottock, four legs as columnars, with short feet standing reect steady. The shape is simple and realistic, the comosition is summarize and overstate, on the vessel adorned with cloud patterns and ogre-dragon designs which are vigorous and graceful. The craftsman used the parts of Ox cleverly, the body as the vessel, the hoof as foot, the tongue as the pouring, rooling the Ox-tail as the handle, opening on the Ox's back for pouring wine into it. The knob of the lid is a tiger in shape, which mixed the artistry and pratical together; shows the expressions of honest, tame and simple; and big pattered designs show the expression of magnificent and artistry.

The experts said that in ancient time, when people held the " Bare Ceremony ", they heeded special vessels, Ox-shape Zun is the wine vessel for the sacrifice.

牛 尊
Ox–shape Zun

日己觥（gōng）

西周中期（公元前10—前9世紀）

通高32cm，長33.5cm，腹深12cm，重9.4公斤

1963年於陝西扶風縣齊家村窖藏出土

此觥通體為一圓雕兇獸，踞在長方座上昂首舒尾。兇雙角呈菌形，菌面飾渦紋，菌莖飾仰覆三角竊曲紋。兇背脊至尾部有扉棱，兩側飾長尾鳳鳥紋。器頸飾回首夔龍幷尾隨鳥紋，腹面飾突起卷角饕餮紋，長方圈足飾鳥紋，座側起扉棱。

日己觥造型奇麗別致，制作精美巧妙。工匠把實用性和藝術性緊密結合，設計渾然一體。兇首為流，腹座為容器，觥體后部以寬大逶迤的尾作把手，足見匠心獨運。

觥是商周貴族宴饗祭祀用的酒器。此觥蓋器各鑄有3行18字銘文，內容記載無名氏為亡父日己鑄造祭器，以庇佑子孫后代。

據郭沫若先生考證：此器是周幽王十一年（前771年）犬戎入侵，西周奴隸主貴族東遷時掩埋。后因歷史變遷，掩埋者未歸或已不在人世，故直到出土，方見天日，成為重要青銅器文物標本。

Ri Ji Gong，a Wine Container

The Mid-Western Zhou Dynasty （10th — 9th century B.C.

H. 32cm. L. 33.5cm, Depth. 12, W. 9.4kg.

Excavated in the pit at Qijiacun, Fufeng County, Shaanxi in 1963.

The vessel is a suanni in shape, monstrous animal in legend which squats on the rectangle base, holding up the head and dangling the tail. Double horns of the animal are mushroom in shape which adorned with whiled designs on the top and triangle ragged curve design on the tems. There are arrises from the back to the tail. Adorned with head-turned ogre-dragon designs and bird designs on the neck "taodie" designs, long-square foot adorned horn-rooled " taotie" designs there are arrises on the bas side.

The shape of this vessel is elegant and unique, casted in smart way and ingeniously. The craftsman linked the artistry and practical tightly, designed unconventionally. The head of the animal as the pouring, the base is the vessel, and the tail of back part is the handle, shows the unique style of casting.

Gong is wine vessel of the feast and sacrifice for the noble. There is an insprition of 3 lines 18 characters both inside the lid and the vessel, its content is about to bless his descendants.

Mr. Guomoruo textual researched that, this vessel was buried by the noble when Quan Rong violiated at the time of King You 11th year （771B.C.）. On the account of changes of history, the nobe who buried the vessel would not come back or died, so up to excavating time, this vessel was seen under the sun again, then became important bronze specimen.

日己觥
Ri Ji Gong, a Wine Container

刖人守門鼎

西周中期

通高17.7cm，口縱橫11.9
×9.2cm，重1.6公斤

1976年於陝西扶風縣莊白
一號窖藏出土

器物上部為鼎，圓角長方形，下部為方座，似居室。侈口，雙附耳，口沿下飾一周竊曲紋，鼎腹素面。鼎上四扉棱作龍形。方座兩側和后面有方格窗，前面有兩扇可啟閉的門，右門扉鑄一抱門刖人。方座四棱下部各有一只鈎嘴圓耳的怪獸，與四足連為一體。

此鼎造型獨特，裝飾華麗，設計別具匠心，是西周中期一件不多見的青銅藝術珍品。鼎扉棱四龍雙角突怒，雙目圓睜，張唇裂嘴，顧首卷尾，前肢蹲伏欲起，后肢撐持有力，體態屈曲，姿勢靈動。門上刖人抱門屈膝，是一個剁去雙腳的奴隸形象。"刖"，就是砍去雙腳，是古代奴隸制時代的一種酷刑。這一"刖人"是西周奴隸制殘酷刑罰的真實反映。

此鼎用于添加炭火溫煮食物。

Square Bronze Tripod for Cooking with the Design of Slave Guarding the Door

The Mid-Western Zhou Dynasty.

*H. 17.7cm, Width 11.9cm * 9.2cm, W. 1.6kg.*

Excavated from the pit No. 1 of Zhuangbai village, Fufeng County, Shaanxxi province in 1976.

The upper part of the vessel is tripod (Ding) with round corner and rectangle, and the lower part is square base which looks like a room. This vessel, flared mouth, two eats, under the edge of mouth, adorned with ragged curves designs in one round, the belly of "Ding" has no design. Four arrises of the "Ding" are dargens is shape. There are square doors which can open in the front, on the left door casted a one-foot slave who holding thebolt. On the base under the four arries, there are four book-shaped mouth-sand round ears animals which kinked with four feet of the vessel.

This shape is unique, decorations are magnificent, designed by supurb mind, it is really a precious bronze gems of Mid-Western Zhou Dynasty. The four dragons on the arrises with projecting horns, goggling eyes opening mouths, head-turned and rolling tails, the limbs are squatting and want to stand, the back limbs prop up steadlly, the shape of the dragon is bending and vivid looking. The shape without foot hold the bolt and bend on his knees, whose feet were choopped off. "Yue" denotes chopping feet off, which is a kind of cruel torture in the time of slave society. This tripod was used for cooking food by charcoal fire.

刖人守門鼎

Square Bronze Tripod for Cooking with the

Design of Slave Guarding the Door

它盉(hé)

西周晚期（公元前9世紀
──前8世紀）

通高37.5cm

1963年於陝西扶風縣齊村
窖藏出土

盉蓋爲一臥姿鷹鷙，雙目圓睜，昂首斂翼，用系環與器身相連。短頸、扁腹，節圓渦紋，周節重環紋、斜角雲紋；流作龍形，張口豎耳；鋬亦作龍形，拱體圈尾，爪連器身；下有四只獸面扁足。蓋內銘一"它"字，故名它盉。

它盉構思巧妙，造型別致，形制輕巧，紋節簡單。器形上的鷹龍，形態活潑矯健，生機盎然。從制作上看，已不再是神秘莊嚴的代表等級和禮制的青銅巨制，也不再有特定濃厚的宗教色彩，更多地表現了迎合世俗需要的形態。是一件反映中國青銅文化發展中由高峰向衰落日漸式微過程中的典型器物。

盉一般用作酒器。祭祀時，將尊中酒倒入盉中，加水調和。也可作水器使用，以盉澆水洗手，以示對祖先和神靈的崇敬。

Ta He，a Wine Vessel

The Late WesternZhou Dynasiy（9th-8th century B.C）

H.37.5cm

Excavated at the pit Qicun，Fufeng County. Shaanxi in 1963

The lid is an eagle in prone position，two eyes goggling，holding head high and wings back，which linked the vessel with a ring. This vessel，short neck，oblate belly which adorned with round whirl designs，ring designs and cloudy designs are on the edge；the pouring pipe is dragon in shape，opening mouth and lifting ears；the handle ia also drangon-shaped，arching its back and rolling its tail，claws closing the vessel；there are four flat feet with animal mask design. Inside the lid，insripited one Chinese Character "Ta"，so called this vessel Ta He.

The plot of this ingeniously conceived，shape is unique，appearance is light and handy，designs are simple. The dragon and eagle，on it are vigorous and graceful. From the casting way，it was not the grand bronze ware which standed for the serious hierarchy and custom system，it has no thick colours of religion. It showed more formation which pandered to common heeding. This is a typical vessel，which mirrored that the development of chinese bronze were down-hill from the peak.

"He" was used as wine vessel generally. When held ceremony，poured the wine vessel generally into the "He" from the Zun，then mixing the wine with water. It also used for holding water，poured water out of "he" and washed hands，that standed reverence for ancestry and gods.

它盉
Ta He, a Wine Vessel

杜虎符

戰國·秦惠文君時期（公元前335——前323年）

通高4.4cm，長9.5cm，厚0.7cm

1973年于陝西西安市南郊山門口出土

虎符因其形而賦名，是我國古代調兵遣將的信物，由帝王授于臣屬。右半在國君，左半在將帥，兩半相符方可調兵。此符鑄成虎形，上有錯金篆書40字。根據秦制，調動五十人以上的軍隊，兩符相合，才能行動。此符刻着"兵甲之符，右在君，左在杜。"即指右符在秦國君王手中，左符為駐扎在杜的將帥所持，故稱"杜虎符"。"杜"在今陝西長安縣。銘文說："燔燧之事，雖毋會符，行殹"，即指若遇緊急軍情，不必會國君的右符，即可舉火行動。

杜虎符小巧精致，形象生動。造型為猛虎疾走形態，寓意為見符如見君，行動要像虎一樣迅捷勇猛。背面有槽，頸上有孔。銘文先鏤刻陰文，再嵌入金絲，打磨光亮，遠望若虎皮斑紋，至今仍閃光如新，燦然生輝。符身錯金銘文反映出二千多年前我國已有高超的錯金工藝水平。三十九字銘文，依虎站立之勢，由頸項開始，從左至右，自然布白，大小不匀，活潑自然。銘文為小篆，瘦勁挺秀，與秦商鞅權量銘文書風近似。史傳小篆為李斯所創，這件杜虎符卻有力證明了小篆在李斯入秦前已很成熟，李斯只是對其作了統一和整理工作。

杜虎符是反映我國古代用兵制度的實物，也是我國現存的最早的虎符。它文字最多，錯金最精，出土最晚，保存又最好，因而文物價值極高。不但對戰國時的政治、軍事史，也對我國的書法篆刻及工藝史的研究，提供了重要的資料。

Tiger Tally with Character of "杜"

In the time of King Hui-wen of Qin State of the Warring states Period (335—323B.C.)

H 4.4cm, L 9.5cm Thickness 0.7cm

Unearthed at Shan MenKou of South Suburb in Xian City, Shaanxi in 1973

Tiger tally got the name of its shape, it's a token by which emporor confered military power on ministers. It was devided into two halves, the right of which was held by the emporor and the left half which was to be held by the commander-in-chief or general, it would be used after two halves were identical. This one casted the shape of tiger, on it is gold-inlaid with 40 characters in the seal style. According to the system of Qin, the dispathing of 50 persons of troop, it must be conformity of two halves, then it would be in effect. On the tally, there is inscription means this tally, the right half was held by the emporor of Qin and the left one was held by the general whose troop was stationed at the place "du". So it was called "du" tiger tally, "du" is at Chang an County in Shaanxi now. Its inscription roughly means in case of emergency, it is allowed to make a sign by fire, not necessary to tally with the right half of the tally.

This tally is small and elegant, shape is vivid. The shape is a fast-walking-tiger, which means seeing the tally as saw the emperor and the action should be as brave and fast as tiger. There is trough on the back and hole on the neck. The characters were carved in intaglio at first, then inlaid gold thread and polished, it is still shinning now and like the stripes of tiger shinning as watching at a distance. Gold inlay characters reflects that China had the high class craft of gold inlay 2000 years ago. Thirty nine characters, according to the tiger erect posture, started from the neck, from the left to the right, with certain space, and were not in the same size which are natural and lively, the style of the character is Xiao Zhuan (a kind of seal), bold and graceful, it was quite like the calligraphy of ShangYang's Quan liang of Qing Dynasty. It was said that Xiao Zhuan was formulated by Lisi but this tally proves that Xiao Zhuan had been ripe befor Lisi in Qin Dynasty, and Lisi just had done some work of patting Xiao Zhuan in order.

This tally is an object which reflects the system of ancient military, is the earliest tiger tally of existing now in China. It has these features, most characters, best gold inlay, excabated last, protect most carefully, so it has the highest value of cultural relic. It supplies important data of researching the politice, military history of the Warring States Period, and calligraphy, seal carving also technological history.

杜虎符
Tiger Tally with Character of "杜"

鳥蓋瓠（hù）壺

戰國時代（公元前475年——公元前221年）

通高33.5cm，口徑5.8cm，圈足徑8.8cm

1967年冬于陝西綏德縣城關公社廢品收購站揀選

此壺形似瓠瓜，蓋為鳥形。鳥首形器蓋以珍珠紋為底，鳥嘴有環扣，可以啟閉。鳥的胸部飾有兩條昂首盤身的蛇紋，尾部有一踏于蛇身伸嘴啄蛇并展翅欲飛的小鳥。瓠壺從肩部至腹部有六道寬帶狀蟠螭紋。肩腹部裝有扁環形把手，把手兩端作龍首形，中部作八棱形。器蓋鳥尾與把手有鏈環連接，鏈環由三節頭朝上、尾巴卷成圓環的蛇紋相互套合。

鳥蓋瓠壺造型新穎別致，紋飾細膩繁褥。六道帶狀蟠螭紋由數百條首尾畢具、若龍若蛇的細小動物交錯纏繞，紛繁多姿，裝飾手法多樣，圖案構思新巧，是青銅器藝術構思從殷周到春秋戰國發展趨勢的體現。

有專家認為，此壺造型為瓠瓜形，象徵"瓠瓜星"。我國古代天文典籍中著錄有"瓠瓜星"，又名"天鷄星"，位于牛郎星以東。壺蓋作鳥首當為"天鷄"無疑。此壺是與祀天有關的盛酒禮器，鳥形裝飾也與秦人的鳥崇拜有關。

Gourd-shaped Pot with a Bird-shaped Lid

Warring States Period (475—221B.C.)

H 37.5cm   D. of mouth 5.8cm   D. of ring foot 8.8cm

Collected from a salvage station at Suide County, Shaanxi in the winter, 1967

The shape of the pot like a gourd, the lid is a bird in shape. One the bird-shaped lid, adorned with pear-pattered designs, with a button in the beak which can open or close. On the chest of bird, adorned with two head-upped and body-rolled snakes designs; on the tail, there is a bird which is pecking the snake and wants to fly from the shoulder to the belly of the pot, there are six wider ribbon-shaped curled Chi-dragon without horns designs. On the belly there is a flat ring-shaped handle two ends of which are dragon heads in shaps, the middle part of the handle is eight-arrise in shape. There is a chain which links up the bird tail and the handle, there are three parts of the chain, each combined with up-head and ring-shaped tail snake.

The shape of the pot is fresh and unique, designs are fine and overelaborate. Six ribbon-shaped dragon designs which formed by hundreds of very fine animals curling and criscrossing; the way of decoration is various and designs are smart and graceful, which is the reflection of bronze developing from Shang, Zhou Dynasties to Warring States Period.

Some experts considers that the shape of gourd symbolized gourd star. It had the record of "gourd star" in Chinese ancient works about astronomy, which star also called "Heaven bird Star", is at the east of altair. The lid is a bird in shape means that is "Heaven Bird". This pot was used for containing wine in the ceremony, design of bird is concerned with worship on bird of Qin people.

鳥蓋瓠壺
Gourd-shaped Pot with a Bird-shaped Lid

銅雁魚燈

西漢（公元前206—公元8年）

通高54cm，長33cm，寬17cm，重4.25公斤

1985年8月於陝西神木縣店塔村出土

雁魚燈為銅質，由一鴻雁回首銜魚構成燈形。雁嘴大張，銜一全魚，魚身巧妙地用作蓋。雁背置一圓形燈盤，盤沿裝一直柄，控制燈盤轉動。燈罩為筒狀，可左右開合，調節燈光照射方向與明暗。燈火點燃后，油烟通過雁頸進入雁體，雁腹盛有水，可將油烟溶入水中，防止了油烟向房內擴散，起到了淨化空氣的作用。雁魚燈由四個部分組成，能自由拆裝，便于清除烟垢。此燈造型生動，設計科學，將實用性和審美性自然結合在一起，形成獨特的樣式。鴨腿直立，鴨蹼展開，支撐着雁體，幷與燈罩、魚蓋、雁首形成中軸，保持了鴨體的穩定。雁頸彎轉回首，自然流暢，與鴨腹渾然一體。雁翅上六條曲綫，平行排列，和雁翅外廓綫走向一致，生動和諧，富有韻律美。

這種雁魚燈全國僅發現兩件，另一件在山西省。

Bronze Lamp in Shape of a Goose Having a Fish in Its Mouth

Weastern Han Dynasty (206B. C. —8A. D.)

Unearthed in August 1985 *at Diantancun, Shenmu County, Shaanxi.*

This is a bonze lamp which is in shape of a head-turned goose having a fish in its mouth. The goose is opening its mouth and holding a fish; the body of fish is the lamp lid cleverly. There is a round lamp plate on the back of goose, with a handle casted on the edge of the plate for controlling the turning of the plate. The lamp-shade is in shape of a tube which can open or close to right or left in order to regulate the direction and brightness of the light. Lighting the oil lamp, smoke of oil goes into the body of the goose from its neck; there is water in the belly of it, then the smoke dissolve in water and not spreads in the room, also purifies the air. The lamp forms with four parts, which can tear open freely and clean the oilblack easily. The shape is vivid, designing is scientific, joining the practical with artstry naturally, which formed the unique syle. The legs of goose are standing straightly, with webs spreading and sustaining the body of goose, which form the central axle with lamp-shade, fish-lid goose-head and keeping the stablity of the goose. The neck of goose turns back and curling, which is graceful and natural, is one integrated mass with the belly. On the wing, adorned with six curves which are in balanced range and in the run with the outline of the wing, they are vivid and harmonious, full of the beautiful of rhyme.

Another lamp like this was excavated in Shaanxi province, there are two pieces only in China.

銅雁魚燈
Bronze Lamp in Shape of a Goose
Having a Fish in Its Mouth

鎏金銅蠶

漢代（公元前206年——公元220年）

長5.6cm，高1.8cm，腹圍1.9cm

1984年12月於陝西石泉縣前池河出土

鎏金銅蠶共有九個腹節，胸腳、腹腳、尾腳完整無缺，仰頭作吐絲狀，體態逼真，制作精致。

這一銅蠶是一農民淘金時挖出的，出土地在陝西南部，古代就是蠶桑盛地。我國養蠶有久遠的歷史，殷墓中出土過玉蠶，商代青銅器上有粘附的精美的絲織遺物，西周墓中也出土過玉蠶，長沙馬王堆一號漢墓出土的一百多件西漢初期的絲織品，都證明這一點。鎏金銅蠶則有力地說明，漢代養蠶風習盛行民間。

像漢代這樣以紅銅鑄造，然后鎏金的蠶在全國是首次發現，也僅此一條，彌足珍貴。它為研究我國蠶桑絲織的歷史和漢代鎏金工藝，提供了珍貴的實物資料。墓中隨葬鎏金銅蠶，具有保佑蠶桑發達之義，也反映了漢代對養蠶業的重視。

Gilt Bronze Silk Worm

Han Dynasty
(206B.C. ——220A.D.)
L 5.6cm   H 1.8cm
1.9cm in girth
Excavated from Qian-chi River at Shiquan County, Shaanxi in december，1984

This gilt bronze silkworm has nine belly joints, with complete feet of chest, belly and tail, holding head high and in shape of spitting silk, which is in vivid looking and in elegant casting.

This bronze silkworm was found by a peasant while he was panning in the river, where is in the south part of Shaanxi and here was a flouring district of raising silkworms in ancient time. China has long history of raising silkworms, we excavated jade silkworm from tomb of Yin Dynasty, and found some magnifiecent silk fabrics which sticked on the bronzes of Shang Dynasty at Mawangdui, Chang-sha city, both of them fully proved this. And this gilt bronze silkwormn gives enough proof of that raising silkworms was popular in the Han Dynasty.

This is the only precious gilt bronze silkworm of Han Dynasty in China. It supplies precious object for the researching of the history of raising silkworms and the technology of gilt of Han Dynasty. Buried the gilt bronze silkworm, which blessed raising silkworms, and also mirrored that Han Dynasty attached importance to raising silkworms.

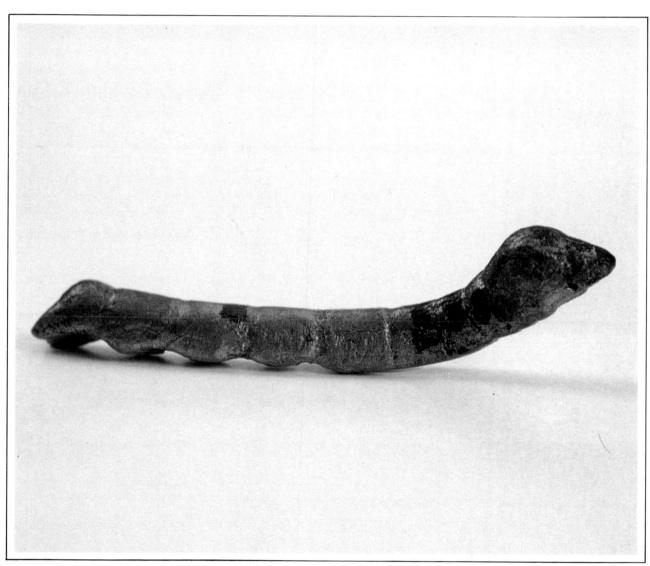

鎏金銅蠶
Gilt Bronze Silk Worm

瑞獸葡萄紋鏡

唐（618—907 年）

直徑 29cm，鏡邊緣厚 1.9cm

1953 年於陝西西鄉縣民間徵集

此鏡圓形。內區有九只瑞獸，形體最大的一只瑞獸居中作獸鈕，其它八只各具形態的瑞獸環繞四周。側旁都有帶枝蔓的葡萄相伴。外區有十六只瑞獸、孔雀、鳳凰、鴛鴦等飛禽走獸相間圍繞，邊緣飾一圈流雲紋。

鏡背紋飾鑄造精美工巧，瑞獸或臥或伏，或嬉戲，或攀援，刻畫細膩。飛禽走獸也形態各異，活靈活現，表現出嫻熟的工藝技巧。

瑞獸葡萄鏡是最具時代意義的唐鏡，它被日本學者稱為"多謎之鏡"，"凝結了歐亞大陸文明之鏡"。瑞獸葡萄鏡大致流行在 7 世紀后半期到 8 世紀前半期，武則天時最為盛行，至開元晚期已近尾聲。由瑞獸和葡萄構成主題紋飾，是把六朝末年在中國已經流行的葡萄紋樣與傳統的瑞獸紋樣結合起來，自由變化的產物。唐代的圖案紋飾處在由瑞獸向花鳥向植物紋飾轉變階段。這一銅鏡工藝之精，紋飾之美，集中體現了一代盛世的文化風貌。而它的形制之大，也是同類鏡中比較罕見的。

銅鏡約在公元前 200 年左右出現，一直到清代玻璃鏡傳入中國，它才作為實用鏡而退出中國舞臺。

此鏡原收藏于西鄉縣一戶官宦人家，可能是一件傳世文物。

Mirror with Lucky-animal and Grape Patterns（Tang Dynasty）（618—907A. D.）

D 18. 7cm, Thickness of edge 1.9cm,

Collected from the people Xixiang County, Shaanxi in 1953

This is a round mirror. There are nine lucky-animal inside the interior circle, and the central biggest one uses as the knob, the other eight ones circling the knob with different pattern. Adornings of grape patterns with branches and tendrils accompanied the animals. In the external circle, circling sixteen birds and animals which lucky-animal alternating with peacock, phoenix and indarin duck, adorned with a circle of flowing cloud designs at the edge.

The designs of the back casted magnificently the lucky-animal are vivid looking in different style, or playing and clibing. The birds and beasts are lively in different patterns which expressed consummate technological skiil.

This mirror with lucky-animal and grape patterns is a tyypical mirror with the significance of Tang Dynasty, which was called "Mirror coagulating the civilization of Eurasia" by Japanese scholars. This mirror was about popular from the late period which was in vogue for a time of the Empress Wuzetian, and closed to the ending at the late period of the time Kai Yuan.

The patterns was unified with traditional lucky-animal designs and grape patterns which was popular at the late period of Six Dynasties, The pattern of Tang Dynasty was in the period which changed the patterns to the birds and plants from lucky-animal, The magnificence of the designs and artistry mirrored the cultural features of flourishing Tang Dynasty. The size of being big is seldom seen in the same kind of bronze mirrors.

Bronze mirror appeared about in 200 B·C·; which did not disappear until the glass mirror entered China in Qing dynasty.

This mirror was collected by an offical family in Xixiang County, which might be a cultual relic handed down from ancient times.

瑞獸葡萄紋鏡
Mirror with Lucky-animal and Grape Patterns

四鸞銜綬帶紋平脫鏡

唐（618—907 年）

直徑 22.7cm，重 1.46 公斤

于陝西西安市長樂坡村出土

此鏡圓形，鏡背分內外區。內區為銀片蓮葉紋，外區為金花鸞鳳綬帶紋。內外區飾兩周金絲同心結紋。這種金銀平脫鏡，是唐代制鏡技術的一種新工藝。其制作方法，是先鑄成有緣無紋的素面鏡，涂上膠漆，然后貼以金銀片制成的各種圖案輪廓，再覆漆研磨，使金銀片與膠漆平齊裸露，隨后精鏤細刻，工藝細若毫髮，便成為平脫鏡。

鏡背四只鸞鳥，口銜長長的綬帶，引頸展翅，若翱翔天宇之中。翅羽分三層，依次整齊鏤出，十分精細華美。鸞鳥形象俊美，婀娜多姿。整個畫面色調和諧、絢麗燦爛，給人富麗優雅之感。這是至今西安地區出土的唐代平脫鏡中最精致、最完整的一面。

鳥銜綬帶，不僅形象優美，還有寓意。"綬"諧音"壽"，表達了吉祥長壽的祝福和願望。同心結紋表示永結同心。這樣的紋飾屬唐玄宗開元以后至唐德宗以前廣為流傳的一種銅鏡紋飾。

Mirror with the Design of Four Birds

Tang Dynasty（618—907）
D. 22.7cm W. 1.46kg.
Unearthed at Changlepo village of Xian City, Shaanxi.

The bank of the round mirror devide interior and extend circle and gold inlaying of lotus designs in the interior circle, and gold inlayings of （Luan）birds （mythical bird like the phoenix）designs both of the interior and external, circling the gold inlayings of heart-shaped chains. This gold and silve inlaid in Tang Dynasty. The method of making was, at first casted a bronze mirror with edge but no designs, painting one layer of lacque, then inlaid the outlines of designs with gold and silver, and then painting more layer of lacque and polishing in order to show the outlines, at last carves all kinds of designs finally, here they got the inlaid and polishing mirror.

The four birs on the back, having the ling ribbon in their mouths hovering in the heaven. Engraving of wings has three layers, which were vigorous and graceful. The postrues of the birds were vivid look and magnificent. The designs are harnonious and bright, which show the expressions of elegance and splendour. This is the most magnificent and complete one of the inlaid mirrors of Tang Dynasty which unearthed in Xian City up to now.

The bold having the ribbon in its mouth, it is not only in pretty shape and with good meaning, the chacatctet "綬" has a harmonym "壽" which is the meaning of long life, heart-shaped chains show being one heart forever, which were popur design on the bronze mirror after Emperor Xuan Zong and before Emperor De Zone in the Tang Dytnasty.

四鸞銜綬帶平脱鏡
Mirror with the Design of Four Birds

獸首瑪瑙杯

唐代（公元 618 年—907 年）

通高 6.5cm，長 15.6cm

1970 年 10 月於陝西西安市南郊何家村出土

這是至今所能見到的唐代唯一的一件俏色玉雕。它造型優美，做工精湛，質地珍貴，是國之瑰寶。此杯選用極為罕見的紅色瑪瑙琢制，兩側深紅，漸漸淡紅，中心乳白，層次明晰，光鮮潤澤。材質紋理細膩，彎曲富于變化，豎直紋理一端被琢成杯口，橫向紋理一端被琢成獸首。獸首圓瞪大眼，目視前方。眼珠黑白分明，神情畢肖。獸角幾度彎曲，粗壯有力，富麗多色。兩只獸耳高高豎起，微微內收。獸頭肌肉，寥寥數刀，生動傳神。整個造型表現出猛獸全神貫注飛馳奔騰的一剎那間的動態美，如一首凝固的詩，一曲流韵的樂章，富有極強的藝術感染力。獸嘴鑲金，金色與獸角和杯口的橙黃色互相呼應，既突出了整體造型的完美，又增添了瑪瑙杯的身價。

此杯的出土地點何家村，是唐代京城長安興化坊的舊地。唐玄宗的堂兄邠王李守禮曾在此坊居住。從大量出土的金銀器和外國貨幣判斷，只有皇親貴戚才可能擁有如此數量的珍寶。而這批珍寶也可能是為躲避安史之亂的叛軍，匆促出逃時埋于地下的。

據專家認為，此杯既象徵著財富，又體現著權力，是一件高貴的藝術品。紅色瑪瑙多產自西域，史書也有康國于開元六年（公元 718 年）遣使給唐朝進獻瑪瑙杯的記載，故出土后曾引起中亞和西亞各國的關注。從目前所知，它是世界同類器物中最精美的一件。

Animal-heart Agate Cup

Tang Dynasty (618—907)

H. 6.5cm, L. 15.6cm.

Excavated at Hejiacun, south surburbs of Xian city, Shaanxi, in Oct. 1970.

This is the only jade carving of Tang Dynasty. Its shape is graceful, crafts is splendid, material precious, it's a rare treasure. The cup was carved with precious agate which is in bright colour and fine veins, the vertical veined part was carve as the cup and the cross wised part was carved as the animal head. The eyes on the head round and goggling. The muscle of head was carved brifly and lively. The shape of this agate cup, is splendid and has grand artistic appear. The mouth is inlaid with gold, the golden is echoing the orange colour of the cup and horns, which is not only showing the splenderour of the shape and provids the status of the agate cup highly.

The place where excavated the cup is Hejiacun, where was old site of Xing hua fang in the Chang'an, the capital of Tang Dynasty. And the King Bin Lishouli, cousin of the Emperor Xuan Zong once lived here. We juged that the cousinship of the Emperor might have so many precious treature from the great deal of gold silver wares and foreign currencies lions which excavated here.

These tresures considered that the cup is a precious gem which symbolized the proper and power. Agate produced from the Western Zhou Regions, there was a recond about that King Kang paid tribute to Emoperor of Tang with this agate cup in 6th year of Kaiyuan (718A·D) in the history book, so it was spectalcul-ared by the cournt ries at Mid-asia and western-asia. After ex-cavating it is the most presious piece of the same kind of wares in the world.

獸首瑪瑙杯
Animal-heart Agate Cup

金怪獸

戰國晚期（公元前 222 年
以前）

通高 11.5cm，長 11cm，重
259 克

1957 年於陝西神木縣納
林高兔出土

金怪獸雙角似鹿，頭面似
馬，彎嘴似鷹，體態似羊，立耳
環眼，遍飾凸雲紋。雙角長過身
軀，向內彎曲，呈八字形向側后
展開。角有四叉，每一叉角頂部
各有一個相似的鷹嘴怪獸頭。
大耳直立，細腰中空，尾部環
卷，獸尾也是一個鷹嘴獸頭。脖
頸屈曲虬結，前肢挺直前傾，后
肢提臀趨前，雙蹄站立在一個
四瓣花形托座上，花瓣周邊各
有三個小圓孔。角、尾和托座另
外範鑄焊接。

通體構思精妙，造型奇特，
生機勃勃，怪异可愛，時隔兩千
多年，仍然金光燦燦，是十分罕
見的純金制品。

此物出土地點在毛烏素沙
漠的南部，戰國時期匈奴民族
常在這一帶活動。從造型上反
映出匈奴人民獨具特色的豐富
想象力和聰明才智，從制造上
表現出北方匈奴地區已經熟練
掌握了捶鍱打印和範鑄焊接的
金屬加工技藝。

這件金怪獸可能是匈奴首
領桂冠上的飾物。

Gold Monster

*Warring State Period
(475—221B·C)*

*H. 11.5cm，L. 11cm
W. 259g.*

*Unearted in Shenmu Coun-
try，Shaanxi in 1957.*

This gold monster is in
stranges ape, horns like deers
head likes a horses, beak like
egle's, and the body like a
sheep, standing ears and round
eyes, adorned with cloud patterns, the horns are longer than
the body of the monster, which
are inwardly curved in a "V"
form streaching backward and
divided into four prongs. On
each tip of the prongs is a lifed
monsterhead which is silmilar
to the monster. The waist of
the monster is hollow, the tail is
in the similar shape of the monster head and curved. The neck
of the monster is bend, front
limbs are straightly standing
forward, back limbs are forward
with the buttock upward, the
hoofs are standing a base which
is in a shape of four-petal flower
with three holes on it's
edge. And the horns, the tails,
and the base holes were casted
separately and then welded together.

The whole shape is in un-
oque style and in vivid look,
after 2000 year, it is still
shiningin splendour, which is a
precious pure gold crafts.

This monster excavated in
the southern part of Mowusu
Desert, where the Huns lived
during the Warring State Period. The shape mirroirs the
unique imagination and wisdom
of the Huns, it is showed that
the Huns had grasped metal
processing.

This gold monster might
be the hanging decoration for
the Hun chief.

金怪獸
Gold Monster

鎏金銀竹節薰爐

西漢中期（公元前153—前106年）

通高58cm，底徑13.3cm，口徑9cm，蓋高6cm

薰爐作高柄竹節豆形，蓋如博山，底座成圈足形，爐體爐柄分鑄鉚合而成，通體鎏金銀。底座透雕兩條蟠龍，仰頭張口，承接五節竹節爐柄。竹節上端三條蟠龍曲體昂首，龍首上承爐盤。爐盤呈半球型，盤口沿有鎏銀寬帶紋一周，下方有十組三角紋，內節鎏金蟠龍。爐蓋透雕層層山巒，呈尖錐狀山形。山巒節有雲氣紋、人物及鳥獸。山下波濤滾滾，四條鎏金顧龍從涌浪中騰出。爐口外側刻有三十五字銘文：“內者未央尚臥，金黃塗竹節薰爐一具，幷重十斤十二兩，四年內官造，五年十月輸，等初三”。從銘文知為宮中之物，是西漢時期一件藝術精品。

這件竹節薰爐為銅質，表層鎏金完好如新，造型華美獨特，工藝精湛考究。據出土地點和銘刻可知，此物是漢武帝劉徹的姐姐陽信公主之物。原在未央宮，后歸陽信家。陽信公主的丈夫是著名史冊的大將軍衛青。

薰爐使用時，在爐內焚香，透過蓋上鏤孔，輕烟繚繞，香氣四溢；蓋上山景朦朧，群獸靈動，高貴雅致，別有風韻。

鎏金是一種手工鍍金方法。它是先將優質黃金打薄成金葉，再剪成細絲，放入潔淨的坩鍋加熱燒紅，然后倒入七倍于金絲重量的水銀，用燒紅的木炭棍充分攪拌，調成泥狀。金泥倒入容器冷却，再倒入一些硝酸，用刀先蘸硝酸，再剗金泥，反復塗抹器物表面。待塗均匀后，又用開水冲洗掉硝酸，再烘烤器物，使水銀揮發掉即成。

A Gilt and Silver Bronze Incence Burner with a Bambon-joint Handle (Mid-Western Han Dynasty) (153—106B·C)

H. 58cm, D. of the base 13.3cm, D. of mouth 9cm, H. of the lid 6cm. Unearthed at Maoling Mausoleun, Shaanxi in 1981.

This burner's body is made by a bowl-shape and with a bamboo-joint handle, its cover is like Boshan (mountain), the plate and the body of the burner are riveted, its whole body is giled with gold and silver. On the base, there are hollowed out two curled dragons with raising bends and opening mouth, bite the bamboo-joint handle. On the top of the handle three curled dragons are cast, their raising heads supporting the plate. The burner is in shape of half-ball, on the edge, giled-ribboned patterns with silver, under which there are 10groups of triangles in which engraved with coiled drangon designs. On the cover of the burnerare open-wrought with peaks cirling with frog and clouds, and also animal and outside the burner are casted 35 inscripitionl characters, recording the date and the weight of the burner. From its inscription, we knew that it is a vessel of the palace which is a gem of the western Han Dynasty.

This is a bronze burner, the girl is as fine as new, the sape is unique and graceful, the technology is splendid. According to the inscription and place of excavating, it was a valauable article for daily use of Princess Yangxin, sister of Emperor Wudi Liuche in the Han Dynasty. It was in the Weiyang Palace originally, then was sent to the pricess Yangxin, whose husband was the famous general WeiQing in history.

When using the burner, burnt the incense inside, and the smoke is curling up from the holes on the cover, then the room will be permeated with fragrance, the designs on the cover are graceful in the fragrant curling smoke.

Gilt is made by hand. At first, beating the pure gold as thin gold leaf, then cutting it into fine threads, heating them into a clean crucible, and pouring it into mercury which is 7times weight of the gold threads, after then mixing as mud with a stick which is burning in res. Then pour the mud into a vessel and cold, pouring some nitric acid, using a kinife dipping in nitric fristly and then scoop the gold mud and painting on the surface of the vessel over and over. After painting evenly, washing out the nitric acid with boiled water, then toasting the vessel in order to volatilize the mercury, the gilt is finished.

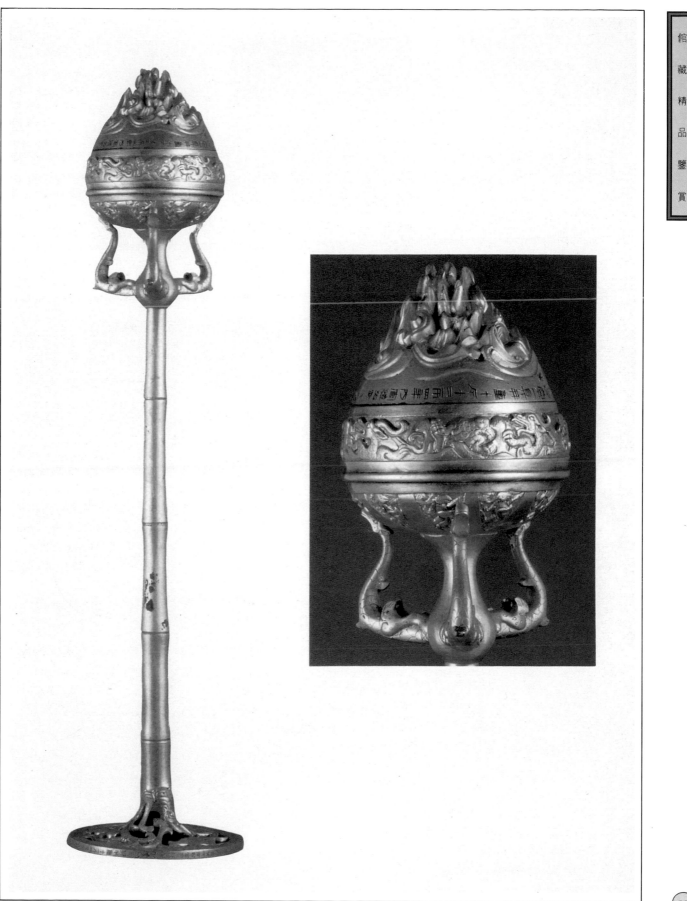

鎏金銀竹節薰爐
A Gilt and Silver Bronze Incence
Burner with a Bamboo—joint Handle

鴛鴦蓮瓣紋金碗

盛唐時期

通高 5.5cm，口徑 13.7cm，足徑 6.7cm

1970 年于陝西西安市南郊何家村窖藏中，出土了1000多件各類文物，其中共有金銀器 270 件，是唐代金銀器出土最多的一次，遠遠超過了全世界收藏的唐代金銀器的總量，引起了國內外學術界極大的興趣。它大大地開闊了研究者的視野，并使早先以傳世品為主的金銀器研究，轉為出土器物為主要研究對象。在 200 多件金銀器中，以兩件鴛鴦蓮瓣紋金碗最為珍貴。

金碗敞口，鼓腹，圈足呈喇叭型，從內壁向外錘擊成型，鏨出兩層浮雕蓮花瓣。上層蓮瓣內鏨有鴛鴦、鸚鵡、獐、鹿、狐、兔等動物，輔之以花草；下層蓮瓣內均作忍冬紋。圈足飾菱形花紋圖案，足底邊緣飾一周蓮珠紋，通身裝飾魚子紋地，顯得富麗典雅。時隔千年，仍金光熠熠，瑰麗無比。它在制作時先將器物劃分成小區間，然后填以適合紋樣，達到美化器物的目的。

金碗內側有墨書"九兩半"三字，標明它的重量。

金碗多為皇帝使用，實物出土極為罕見，史料記載也不多。從現有資料看，它是唐代金銀器中僅見的最堂皇的金碗。這一實物代表了盛唐時期我國北方金銀器制作的高度成就。

Gold Bown with Designs of Mandarin Dusks and Lotus

Tang Dynasty.

H.5.5cm，D. of mouth 13.7cm，D. of ring foot 6.7cm.

Then toasting the vessel in order to volatrilize the mercury, the gilt is finished.

One thousand pieces of culture relics were unearthed at the pit of Heijiacun, at the south surburbs of Xian City in 1970, of which there were 270 pieces of gold and silver wares, it was the first time of excave ting gold and silver wares of Tang Dynasty, the collection with gold and silver wares of Tang Dynasty, went beyond the quatities of it in the world. This was noticeable in the sphere of learning, which widened the sight of research worker, and changed the object of researching on the unearthed vessels from the handed down wares of gold and silver. Among the 270 pieces of gold and silver wares, two gold bowls with designs of mandarin ducks and lotus are most precious.

The mouth of the bowl is flared, the belly building, the ring foot is in shape of bell, two close layes of relief lotus petal patterns are chiselled from the interior to outer walls of the belly. The upper layer of lotus patals is decorated with branches of flowers and there are mandarin ducks, parrots, deers, foxes etc. Dotted among them; rose designs are chiselled on the lower layer of lotus and the edge of it is decorated with chains of rings. The whole wall are decorated with peal patterns, showing splendour and elegance. After thousand year, it is still shinning and graceful.

Inside the bowl is mostly for the Emperor dairly use, the object is seldom seen, and less recorded in the historical books. According to the date, it is the most precious and splendid gold bowl of the gold and silver wares in the Tang Dynasty. This object symbolizes the achievment of gold and silver making in the northeren of China of the flourishing Tang Dynasty.

鴛鴦蓮瓣紋金碗
Gold Bown with Designs of Mandarin Ducks and Lotus

舞馬銜杯紋銀壺

盛唐時期
通高 18.5cm，口徑 2.3cm
1970 年 10 月於西安南郊
何家村窖藏出土

銀壺為皮囊式馬蹬型，壺口在扁圓形壺身頂端一角，呈豎筒狀，上置覆蓮瓣式壺蓋。蓋頂和弓形壺柄由一麥穗銀鏈連接，壺身下端焊有橢圓形圈足。壺身兩面各有一個模壓凸出的作騰躍匐拜的銜杯舞馬。

唐玄宗李隆基在位后期，曾親自訓練舞馬。每年八月初生日時，舞馬被披錦掛玉，按樂曲節拍跳舞祝壽。開元 18 年（公元 730 年），宰相張說親睹過祝壽場面，并寫了一首《舞馬千秋萬歲樂府詞》："聖皇至德與天齊，天馬來儀自海西。腕足徐行拜兩膝，繁驕不進踏千蹄。鬤鬃奮鬣時蹲踏，鼓怒驤身忽上躋。更有銜杯終宴曲，垂頭掉尾醉如泥。"詩中所描述的曲終情景與銀壺上所表現的舞馬神態十分吻合。唐代工匠選用舞馬曲終的舞姿，加以藝術化處理，讓它前腿直立，后腿曲膝，鬤鬃系上彩帶，突出一個屈膝銜杯的舞馬形象，顯得馴養有素，靈動可愛。

皮囊式壺，在唐代金銀器中是首次見到，考古學家一般把這一形制的壺當作契丹文化的代表器物。在原唐代長安京城出土皮囊式馬蹬銀壺，是漢民族和契丹文化交流的明證。

此壺采用隱起鏨花手法，造型匠心獨運，形制特殊，花紋精美。銀白色的壺上，舞馬、壺蓋和提梁，均鎏上一層黃燦燦的金色，與壺體銀色交相輝映，色調格外和諧富麗。從工藝水平上看，它是唐代工匠的傑出之作。

Silver Pot with Design of Dancing Horse Holding a Cup in Its Mouth

Tang Dynasty（618—907A·D)
H. 18.5cm，D. of mouth 2.2cm
Unearthed at the pit of Hejiacun, Xian city, Shaanxi in Oct·1970

The silver pit is leather-bag style and in the shape of a stirrup the mouth is at the top corner of the flat body of the pot，which is in the shape of a vertical tube，there is a lotus-petal-shaped cover on it. Asilver chain is linking the cover and the bow-shaped handle，the oval ring foot is welbed under the body of piot. Each side of the belly，there is a raised dancing horse holding cup in its mouth.

When the Emperor Xuan-Zong Lilongji was at the throne，who trained the horse to dance by himself. At the birthday ceremony in August each year，dancing horse was decorated with jade and brocade，dancing for the birthday celebration allow the rhythm of music. In 18th year of Kaiyuan（730A. D)，the prine minister Zhangyue took part in the celebration and wrote apoem which was about the dancing horse for the emperor's birthday ceremony. In the poem，describing the dancing horse in a similar posture of the design on the pot. The crafts man chosed posture of the end of the music，dealing with artry，the front legs standing erectly，the back limbs bending the knees，tying ribbon to the mane showing the dancing horse with up，which is in vivid look and graceful.

Leather-pag-styled pot，it is the first time to see in the gold and silver ware of the Tang Dynasty；generally，the archeaologists regard this style pot is the typical vessel of the khitan's culture. This silver pot which excavated in the capital of Tang Dynasty，which is the cerficate of culture exchange between the Han nationality and the khitan.

This pot used the method of raised chiseling，the style is unique and the designs are vigourous，on the silver pot，dancing horse，the cover and the handle are gilblid with golden，which makes the designs in the harmonious and splendid style. Accouting to the craft. It's a outstanding piece of the crafrsman in the Tang Dynasty.

舞馬銜杯紋銀壺
Silver Pot with Design of Dancing Horse
Holding a Cup in Its Mouth

樂伎八棱金杯

唐（公元 618—907 年）

高 6.cm，口徑 7.2cm

1970 年於陝西西安何家村窖藏出土

金杯杯身八棱，侈口，腹下折內收為圓底，圈足呈喇叭型，足沿為環狀聯珠。環形柄上為一對浮雕胡人頭，后腦相連，高鼻深目，長髯下垂。杯外側有獸頭，柄下出鈎尾。

杯身八棱用聯珠為欄界，每棱浮雕一伎樂人物，或手執拍板，或敲打小鐃，或彈奏琵琶，或吹奏洞簫。另外四人或抱壺，或執杯，或空手起舞。八人均系頭戴卷檐尖帽或瓦楞帽的胡人。

此杯先澆鑄成型，后用平鏨手法雕鏨細部，人物周圍則飾以山石飛鳥、忍冬卷草和翩翩蝴蝶。杯底鏨八朵忍冬花結。

據專家研究認為，樂伎八棱金杯的環形柄上焊有胡人頭象平鏨，"是初唐金銀器受波斯薩冊朝銀器影響的顯證。"人物紋樣寫實性很強，是對唐代貴族娛樂活動的真實寫照。

Gold Octagonal Cup with Muscians and Jugglers Design

Tang Dynatsy (618—907A·D)

H. 6.4cm, D. of mouth 7.2cm.

Unearthes in the pit of Hejiacun city, in 1970.

The body of the cup is octagon, with a flared mouth, the lower belly contracted inward being the round bottom, the ring foot is a bell in shape, on the edge of the foot with chains of rings. On the top of the ring-handle engraved Humen heads back to back, with high noses, hollow eyes, and long beard.

The octagon of the cup is devided with chains of rings, each side of the cup carved with one figure, one handing, sounding-boards, one playing xiao (verticalflute); the other four figures; or holding pot or cup, and dancing. They are Hu man with different style caps.

This gold cup was cast in shape firstly. Then chiselled the designs adorned with the birds. honeysuckle and butterflies beside the figures. On the base of the cup, chiselled with the honeysuckle-flower designs.

According to the heads of Hu man on the ring-shaped handle, the experts considered that, it was the proof of the gold, silver wares of early Tang Dynasty influenced by the silver wares of Sasanian period of persia. The designs of the figures mirror the entertainment of the nolbleman in the Tang Dynasty.

樂伎八棱金杯
Gold Octagonal Cup with Musicians and Jugglers Design

金框寶鈿團花金杯

唐（618—907 年）

高 5.9cm，口徑 6.8cm，足徑 3.5cm

1970 年于陝西西安市南郊何家村窖藏出土。

此杯金質，口略敞，束腰，短足，環柄，帶翹尾，杯腹內為素面，腹外焊接有以金絲編成的四朵薔薇式團花，團花周邊鑲一圈魚子紋。花瓣中心曾鑲有寶鈿真珠，出土時已脫落。杯沿下及底沿上，各有四朵金絲編成的如意雲頭。

此杯為飲酒器，制作精巧，光彩奪目，系澆鑄后切削成型。切削加工的紋路清晰細密，金絲焊接處焊口平直，技巧純熟，不露焊縫。團花紋飾富有民族特色，在紋飾布局和結構上，周密地考慮了器物的整體和局部的關係，是唐代金銀器制作工藝成熟完美的代表作之一。

Gold Cup with Posy Designs

Tang Dynasty （618—907A・D）

H. 5.9cm・D. of mouth 6.8cm，D. of foot 3.5cm.

Unearthed from the pit of Hejiacun, Xian City, Shaanxi, in 1970.

This is pure gold cup. with a flared mouth, hollow waist of the belly short ring foot, ring-shape handle with a tail upward, inside the belly without design, on the wall of the belly, welbed four posy designs which wove in gold read and in rose style, on the edge of the posy design, inlaid chains of rings patterns. In the middle of the poay design, once inlaid the peart, but fell off as excavated. Under the edge of the mouth and on the lower edge of the belly, each decorated with four lucky cloud patterns.

This is a wine vessel, it is a shining elaborately wrought gold ware, which is modeled by chopping after cast. The veins of chopping is clear and fine, the welbing of gold thread is skillful and brilliant. The pattern of posy is rich of national feature, the arrangment of the designs and the form are thought over carefully with the relationship of whole and the part. It is a masterpiece of pefect gold and silver wares of the Tang Dynasty.

金框寶鈿團花金杯
Gold Cup with Posy Designs

仕女狩獵紋八瓣銀杯

唐（公元618—907年）

高5.1cm，口徑9.1cm，足徑3.8cm

1970年于陝西西安市何家村窖藏出土

銀杯呈八瓣花形。杯口為八曲形，窄平折沿，小聯珠唇，弧腹，腹下緣有八瓣仰蓮，喇叭形八棱圈足，足沿由球狀聯珠綴成。杯柄平鏨，呈如意雲頭，上鏨花角鹿紋，柄下有鈎尾。

杯身依八瓣造型自然劃分為八個裝飾區間，平鏨出仕女和狩獵的各種生活紋樣。仕女或樂舞，或閑游，或戲嬰，或梳妝；男子或狩獵，或逐鹿，或馳驅，或射殺，生動地刻劃出唐代貴族婦女的日常生活面貌，同時，也再現了上流社會崇尚射獵的真實情景。

銀杯上的仕女狩獵紋樣涂成金色，襯以魚子紋地。整個器物造型優美，玲瓏可愛，通體華貴，風格高雅。工匠錘擊成型時，能從統一中求變化，從規整中顯活潑，用弧綫和曲折使器物表現出節奏感和韵律美。對人物和場景的描摹，點畫不多，妙得其真，反映出工匠對現實生活觀察得細致入微，表現得又千姿百態。從杯身仕女的發髻，可知這是唐代開元時的典型發式，說明銀杯為開元時或開元之后所制。裝飾紋樣充分顯示了唐代工藝達到的高度成就。

Silver Octagonal Cup with Figure and Hunting Design

Tang Dynasty（618—907A. D）

H. 5.1cm，D. of mouth 9.1cm，D. of foot 3.8cm.

The silver cup is the octagon-petal in shape. The mouth is in eight-camber shape，narrow flat edge with the chains of rings，the belly is arc in shape，the lower part of the belly adorned with eight-petal lotus design，octagonal bell-shape ring foot，the edge of foot decorated with the chains of rings. Flat handle is in lucky-cloud shape which is on the ring-handle，with a curled tail under the ring.

Each side of the octagonal belly，carved the patterns of female figure and hunting. the female figures are dnacing. playing，or making up；the male figures are hunting，riding，withbow and arrow，chasing the deer，which vivdly mirror the daily life feature of the noble women and the worship hunting among the high society.

The designs on the belly of the silver cup，are gilded in gold，adorned with pearl patterns. The shape is graceful，which is lively and in elegant style. The crafts man made it in octagonal shape which showed the thythm and splendour. Designs of the figure and hunting simply mirror the fantanstical imagination and observing finely of the crastsman. According to the hairstyle in the Kaiyuan Period of the Tang Dynasty，symbolized that the silver cup was made at that time or after that period. The designs are proof of that the crafts in Tang Dynasty has achieved high level.

仕女狩獵紋八瓣銀杯
Silver Octagonal Cup with Figure and Hunting Design

雙獅紋單柄金鐺

唐（公元618—907年）

高3.4cm，口徑9.2cm，柄長3cm

1970年于陝西西安市何家村窖藏出土

金鐺敞□，翻沿，淺腹，圓底，三獸足。鐺□沿下裝一單柄，呈葉芽狀。器外自底部中心凸起九條荷葉脈，呈"S"型彎轉，直通器□，自然分成九個斜形區間，區內飾以蔓草、鴛鴦、花卉等紋樣，間隙飾珍珠紋底。器內底部飾以栖息的雙獅。三獸足上部若虎頭，□內伸出虎爪，組成鐺足。

鐺是古代一種三足溫酒器。此鐺赤金，錘擊成型。花紋陰綫平鏨，紋飾配置靈活。雙獅采用浮雕手法，造型十分可愛。此鐺單柄設計成葉芽狀，用游動的曲綫帶給器物以生機，克服了造型的呆滯死板。整個金鐺做工精細，焊縫光滑，鏨刻細膩，裝飾富麗，光澤熠熠，是一件堂皇考究的唐代宮庭金器。

Gold Cheng with a Handle and Double-lion Pattern

Tang Dynasty（618—907A·D）

H. 3.4cm，D. of mouth 9.2cm，L. of handle 3cm.

Unearthed at Hejiacun, Xian city, Shaanxi in 1970.

This gold cheng has a flared mouth, rolling edge, shallow, belly, round bottom, three animal-shaped feet. There is a leaf-shaped handle unearthed the edge. On the outer wall of the belly, raised carring 9 veins of lotus-leaf, in a "s" shape curling to the mouth of the veesel, devided the belly into 9 parts, adorned with the designs of mandarin ducks and flowers etc. inside the part, and carved pearl pattern at the deviding line. Inside the vessel, engraved double-lion pattern The upper part of the foot like tigers head, claw out of the mouth three feet like this supporting the vessel.

Cheng is a kind of veesel for warming up the wine with three feet in ancient time. This piece is pure gold, made by har-

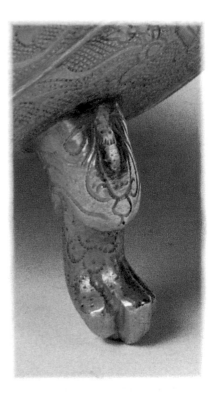

mmer, the designs are chislled in intaglic, which are greceful and delicate. the double-lion carved in relief, which is lively and pretty good. The handle is designed in a leaf-shape, which supply the life to the vessel with the curve. The making of this gold cheng is fine, welbing is perfect chiselling is splendid, decration is properous, which is a rare gold vessel of the Royal in the Tang Dynasty.

雙獅紋單柄金鐺
Gold Cheng with a Handle and Double—lion Pattern

鸚鵡紋提梁銀罐

唐（公元618—907年）

高24.2cm，口徑12.4cm，足徑14.3cm，重1879克

1970年于陝西西安市何家村窖藏出土

銀罐大口短頸，罐腹圓鼓，以折枝花圍繞鸚鵡，組成均衡式圓形圖案，頸與足均飾海棠四出花瓣。提梁插入焊接在肩部的兩個葫蘆形附耳內，可自由活動。蓋心飾一朵寶相團花，蓋面周圍飾石榴、葡萄及忍冬卷草，提梁飾菱形圖案。

此罐錘擊成型，平鏨花紋，紋樣鎏金，魚子紋襯地。器形通體裝飾紋樣，結構巧致，富麗華貴，圓渾可愛。處于中心位置的鸚鵡圓睛含神，鈎喙銳爪，振翅欲飛，栩栩如生。圍繞四周的折枝花葉，俯仰自然，繁簡得當，綫條圓活，枝蔓流暢。邊飾和余白花葉，布局工巧謹嚴，底紋細密勻稱，裝飾意味濃厚。表現了金銀工匠高超的藝術造型能力和精湛的平鏨技巧，反映了唐代工匠純熟的捶揲水平和創造才情。

銀罐蓋內原有一行墨書："紫英五十兩"、"石英十二兩"，表明為收藏中藥的器具。這類器具是盛唐時期新出現的器形，生機盎然的罐腹雕飾，蘊含祈求康寧、幸福和長壽之意。

Silver Jar with Parrot Design

Tang Dynast （618—907）

H. 24.2cm, D. of mouth 12.4cm, D. of foot 14.3, W. 1879g

Unearthed at Hejiacun, Xian City, Shaanxi, 1970.

This silver jar, with wide mouth, short neck, belly is bulged, decorated the parrot design which is circling the flowers designs; on the neck and foot, adorned eight designs of chinese flowering crabapple. The beam was welbed in the two bottle gourd-shape ears on the shouder of the jar, which can turn freely. Posy design is adorned in the middle of the cover, on the cover, engraved the patterns of pomegranate, grape and honeysuckle, the beam is adorned with thombs design.

This jar is hammered into shape, chislling the design which is gilded of gold, decorating with pearl pattern, the designs on the body are greceful and splendid forming lively. The parrot in the central with round eyes, curled beak and sharp claws, wings are flying, which is life like. The patterns of flowers enclosing the parrot are natural and greceful, which shows the square class abilities and craftsman whose designing and chiselling; it is also mirriores the lever of hammering into sharp of the craftsman in the Tang Dynasty.

There are character of "Zi" Ying 50 taels, ShiYing 20 taels inside the cover originally, which might be a vessel for collecting the Chinese medicine. This kind of vessel was a new shape of the vessels in the flourisning Tang Dynasty, and the vigourous designs contain the meaings of peace, happiness and long life.

鸚鵡紋提梁銀罐
Silver Jar with Parrot Design

鎏金雙狐紋雙桃形銀盤

唐（公元618—907年）

通高1.5cm，口徑22.5cm

1970年于陝西西安市南郊何家村窖藏出土

銀盤為雙桃形，寬邊，淺腹，平底。盤內捶出凸起雙狐。雙狐鎏金。一狐側身仰首，尖嘴上伸，目光逼視對方，拱腰作行走狀，長尾下垂；一狐側身彎首，尖嘴前伸，雙目緊盯對方，前肢微蹲，后肢蹬地，作警惕欲鬥狀，長尾下拖。雙狐首尾錯置，顧盼生姿，神態逼真。

在唐代，狐同龍、鳳、獅、犀、熊、鹿、兔等一樣，均屬祥瑞之獸。"百姓多事狐神"，以祈求平安。據載，唐代有"無狐魅，不成村"的諺語流傳，這大概是銀盤用狐紋作裝飾的原因。

此銀盤造型優美，做工精細，展示了唐代金銀器工藝的嶄新風貌。這種金花素底銀盤，用動物圖案作裝飾，圖案凸起，具有浮雕效果，從造型到紋飾帶有濃厚的波斯薩珊王朝藝術風格的影響。同窖還出土裝飾着熊、龜、鳳馬牛怪獸等紋樣的銀盤，是唐代手工業的發展水平和對外來技藝大量吸收的物證。

Gilt Silver Plate in Double-peach Shape and with Double-fox Designs

`Tang Dynasty`（618—907A. D）

H.1.5cm，D. of mouth 22.5cm.

Unearthed from the pit of Hejiacun, Xian, Shaanxi, in 1970.

The silver plate is in double-peach shape, wide edge, shallow belly and flat bottom. Inside the plate, hammered raised double-fox which are gilt. One of the fox is holding up head, extending the mouth upward, staring at the other one, which arched in its back and in runing shape, dangling its tail; the other one is turning down its head, put the mouth forward, glazing at the opposite one, with a shape in being fighting, dangling tail.

In the Tang Dynasty. the fox dragon, phoenix, lion, rhinoceros, deers, bear etc, were regarded as the lucky animals. The people blessed peace with attending upon the fox deity. A proverb "being Not a village, village without " Fox Deity" was spreading widely in the Tang Dynasty, which might be the reason of decorating with for pattern.

This silver plate is in perfect shape, make finely, which shows the new feature of the crafts of gold wares in the Tang Dynasty. This clean bottom with gilt animal design which is raised as relief; according to the shape and design, influenced by the art setle by the sasanian period of Pesia. We excavated some silver plate with bear, turtle, phoenix, horse etc. designs at the same pit. which are proof of that the developing of handicraft in the Tang Dynasty absorb a large number of crafts abroad.

 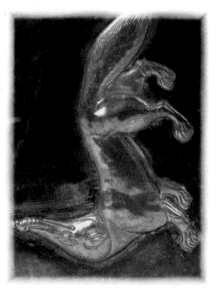

鎏金雙狐紋雙桃形銀盤
Gilt Silver Plate in Double-peach
Shape and with Double-fox Designs

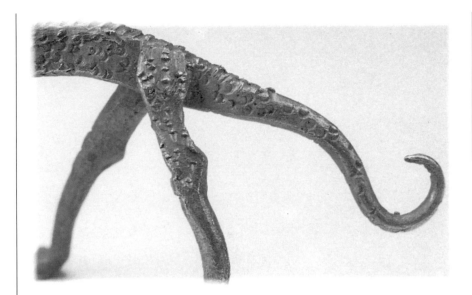

赤金走龍

唐　（公元618—907年）

高2cm，長約4cm

1970年陜西西安市南郊何家村窖藏出土

走龍用純金制成，體形小巧，神情畢肖。龍首高昂，尾部舒卷，軀體修長，四肢勁健。圓眼深目，兩唇開張，造型生動，刻劃精微，周身鱗片，一絲不苟。從龍頭到背脊，到尾部，形成一條優美流暢的曲綫，四肢若奔若走，各現其姿，宛若群龍相邀，悠閑出遊。

龍在自然界里并不存在，龍的形象是多種動物特征綜合想象的創造。在遠古時代，龍最初是雷電雲雨之神，雷電主宰雲雨，雨水決定豐歉，含有祈祝天地和合，風調雨順，五谷豐登的涵義。龍作為雷雨之神，最早產生于中原地區。1987年，在河南濮陽縣西水坡遺址仰韶文化早期墓葬里，發現用蚌殼在地面擺塑而成的龍的形象，是目前所見時代最早的龍的形象，距今約六千多年。漢代時的人認為："龍，鱗蟲之長，能幽能明，能細能巨，能短能長。春分而登天，秋分而潛淵。"事實上，龍是以農為本的中華民族的祥瑞之神，也是中華民族及其文化的藝術象征。而在漫長的封建社會里，它被歷代王朝賦予特殊的含義，成為帝王的象征。

赤金走龍出土時共有十二個，個個精美，玲瓏可愛。

Gold Dragon in Running State

Tang Dynasty (618—907)

H. 2cm, L. 4cm.

Unearthed from the pit at Hejiacun, Xian, Shaanxi in 1970.

The running dragon is made by pure gold, small and exquisite in shape and vivid in looking. Head of dragon is holding high, the tail is rolling, he body is slender, the limbs are healthy and vigourous; which has two round eyes, opening the lips, life like shape and engraved finely scale. There is a graceful curve from the neck to the back and up to the tail, the four limbs are in running or walking with different posture, just like the host of dragons running leisurely and carefree.

Dragon does not exit in the life, it is created by the imagination which is unified with many kinds of animals features. In remote antiquity, dragon was the god of thunder, cloud and rain originally, the thunder dominate the cloud and rain, and the rain decided the harvest, which is meaning of blessing harvest, and favourable weather. Being the God of the thunder and rain, dragon was produced earliest in the central plains. In 1987, in the tombs of early Yangshao culture in Puyang County, Henan, Unearthed a dragon which was molded with the shall of dam, it is the earliest style of dragon, about six thousand years ago. In fact, the dragon is the lucky-god which is blessing the agriculture of Chinese, and it is also the symbol of the Chinese culture and Chinese nationality. But in the Long feudal society, the dragon became the symbol of the emperor with the special meaning.

We unearthed twelve dragons like this, each is likely and vigorous.

赤金走龍
Gold Dragon in Running State

鏤空飛鴻球紋銀籠子

晚唐懿宗李漼咸通15年（公元874年）入藏法門寺地宮

通高 17.8cm，口徑16cm，腹深 10.2cm，1987年4月在陝西扶風縣法門寺真身寶塔地宮中現世。

籠子通體鏤空，作球紋，紋飾鎏金，帶蓋，直口，深腹，平底，四足，有提梁。蓋為穹頂，口沿下折與籠體扣合，頂面模沖有十五隻飛鴻，內圈五隻引頸向內，外圈十隻兩兩相對，蓋邊緣飾蓮瓣紋樣。下緣一周飾一正一倒排列的蓮花，蓮花周圍填滿魚子紋底。籠體腹壁鏨有二十四隻飛鴻，兩兩相對，三層間格排列。兩側鉚有環耳，環耳上套置提梁和銀鏈，銀鏈與蓋頂相連。每足為與籠底邊緣鉚接的"品"字形花瓣。

鏤空飛鴻球紋銀籠子是焙茶用的籠子，用作烘去茶葉的濕氣。唐代制茶，據陸羽《茶經》所載，需晴日采茶，然後經蒸、搗、拍、焙、穿、封等幾道工序，制成團茶或餅茶。故飲茶前，須將團餅用淨紙密裹搥破，然後碾碎過羅，再投入沸水烹煮。為使團餅存放干燥而色香不減，必須放入吸熱方便又易于散發水氣的焙籠中。

籠子經錘揲、模沖成型。整個器物玲瓏剔透，精致典雅。工整排列的球紋與飛動的鴻雁形成靜與動的強烈對比。鴻雁神態逼真，攜伴翔舞，相對引頸，似唱似語，達到了實用性與藝術性的完美結合，也可領悟到唐代皇室飲茶的精細和奢華。

Openwork Silver Cage with Gilt Swan Goose and Lotus Design

Hidden in the underground palace of Fameng Temple In the 15th year of Xian Tong（874A. D），late Tang Dynasty.

H. 17.8cm，D. of mouth 16cm，Depth of belly 10.2cm.

Unearthed from the underground palace of Famen Temple，Fufeng County Shaanxi，in April 1987.

The whole body of this cage is hollowed out with ball-pattern，with gilt designs，with a cover，deep belly，flat bottom，four feet a beam. The lid is an arched roof，and the edge turn down and fit for the body，fifteen geese are punched on the lid. Along the interior rim five geese are streching their necks inward，while along the outer ten-petal design on the edge of the lid. The lower edge of the lid，adorned with symmtrical lotus designs，filling with the pear-pattern. Three layers of twenty four geese are Chiselled on the belly，streching their necks and spreding wings int wos. On the two sides are riveted ears in the shape of ring，connected with a beam and silver chain，and the silver chain conncted with the top of thelid，under the body，rieted "v" from petal design as the foot.

This silver cage is for sying tea.

The cage is hammered and punchedins shape，the whle cage is made exquistely，unique and elegent. The neat ball patterns with the flying geese designs，which form a sharp contcast. The geese are life like，flying with the partners，streching their necks in twos，which is unified the practical with artistry perfectly，at the same time we comprehend that the tea in Tang imperial is fine and luxury.

鏤空飛鴻球紋銀籠子
Openwork Silver Cage with Gilt
Swan Goose and Lotus Design

蔓草鴛鴦紋銀羽觴

唐　（公元618—907年）

高 3cm，口 徑 10.5 × 7.7cm，底徑6.6×4.2cm

1970年于陝西西安市何家村唐代窖藏出土

羽觴是古代飲酒用的耳杯。古人或以羽觴酌飲，如《漢書·孝成班倢伃傳》有："酌羽觴兮銷魂"；或以羽觴雅聚，如王羲之《蘭亭序》就有"曲觴流飲"。這件銀羽觴提供了宮庭羽觴的眞實形象。

銀羽觴呈橢圓形。有長方形片狀雙耳，焊于口沿之下。器內底心飾一朵海棠，內壁刻有四株折枝蓮，花盛葉碩，枝蔓流暢；間飾流雲紋，雙耳面各刻一朵小團花。耳下外腹各刻一組抱合式蓮花卷草紋，覆座上各立一只鴛鴦，一側爲振翅，一側爲斂翼。兩端外飾一對振翅立式鴛鴦，下有覆蓮座。器身滿飾珍珠地紋，紋飾平鏨涂金，華麗异常。一件羽觴上，共刻畫了六只神態各异的鴛鴦，和團花卷草相映成趣，充滿祥和生機。

在唐代金銀器上，鴛鴦圖案非常普遍。由于鴛鴦具有成對生活的習性，被人們視爲對愛情專一、忠貞不渝的象征。這件羽觴大約用于宮庭婚宴喜慶之時。

一件小小的羽觴，采用了鈑金、澆鑄、焊接、拋光、錘鍱、刻鏨、鎏金等工藝，制作精巧，焊縫嚴密，刻鏨精湛，鍍金高超，顯得高雅華貴。旣有實用性，又具欣賞價値。

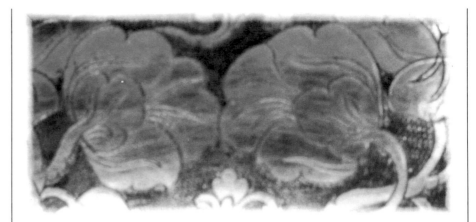

Silver Wine Cup（yu shang）with Mandarin Duck Pattern

Tang Dynasty.（618—907A. D）

H. 3cm, D. of mouth 10.5 ×7. 7cm, D. of foot 6.6× 4.2cm.

Unearthed at Hejiacun, Xian City, Shaanxi in1970.

Yu shang is a kind of cup for drinking wine in ancient time. Ancient people drunk wine with it, and also made elegant gather while playing game with it.

This silver Yushang is oval, with two rectangle flake ears, which are under the edge of its mouth. Inside the cup, in the center of bottom adorned with a Chinese flouring crabapple design; on the interior wall engrave four lotus designs, decorating with floating cloud designs; on the double ears, engraved with posy designs. Under each ear, engraved group of lotus designs, on which standing eings, and the other is closing wings. Each side of the belly, adorned with standing double-mandarin duck design, under which is lotus design and filling with peal-pattern. The designs are chiselled and gilt, splendid and graceful. In this cup, altogether carved six mandarin decks in different poature, decorated with posy designs forming a delightful contrast, which is full of propositions life.

The mandarin duck design was very popular design on the gold and silver wares in the Tang Dynasty. On account of the habits and characterisitc of mandarin duck living in double, which were regared as the symbol of being constant in love. This silver poece might be using for the wedding ceremony of the Royal.

This small silver cup, made with casting, welding, polishing, hammering, chiselling etc. crafts, which is splendid and elegant with the magnificent made. It has practical and value of appriatation.

蔓草鴛鴦紋銀羽觴
Silver Wine Cup (yu shang) with Mandarin Duck Pattern

刻花鎏金鸞鳳紋銀盤

唐 （公元618—907年）

口徑55cm

1962年3月于陝西西安市
北郊坑底寨出土

銀盤盤底呈六曲形，盤心折枝花團中，一對鸞鳳展翅翔翔。鳳尾舒卷，迤邐展成半圓，幾與另一隻鳳鳥的右翼相接。翅羽和絨毛鏨刻精細，似乎在花叢翔舞中隨風游動。環繞鸞鳳一周的有六朵小簇團花，三株向心，三株輻射，間隔排列。盤治飾六組扁團花，每組之間飾雙鳥啣花或雙鳥銜蝶，和諧與共，結伴飛舞。整個銀盤外廓也略呈六曲，花紋平鏨，紋飾塗金，花鳥相間，金銀交錯，裝飾富麗，華美精致。

銀盤背面有銘文三行四十一字：“浙東道都團練觀察處署等使”，“大中大夫守越州刺史兼御史大夫上柱國賜金魚袋臣裴肅進”，“點過訖”。裴肅其人，據《資治通鑑》載：“浙東觀察使裴肅旣以進奉得進，判官齊總代掌后務，刻剝以求媚又過之”。此銀盤即為裴肅向唐德宗李適進獻的禮物之一，為史書提供了實證。進獻時間當在唐德宗貞元十五年（公元799年）至貞元十九年（公元803年）之間。

Gilt Silver Plate with Phoenix Design

Tang Dynasty. （618—907A. D.）

D·of mouth 5.5cm,

Unearthed at Kengdizai, north suburb of Xian City in March，1962.

This silver plate's bottom is hexagonal arched, in the central posy patterns of bottoms, adorned with gilt double-phoenix design, the double-phoenix design streching their wings and hoveing. The wings and feather are chiselled very finely, which like move about as the wind blowing. There are six-posy patterns circling the phoenix. On the dege of the plate, decorated with six froup of posy patterns, among each group, adorned with different style patterns of double-bird. The outline of the plate is hexagonal, with gilt chiselled designs of birds and flowers, decorted splendidly and which is graceful.

On the back of the plate, there is a insprition of 3 lines and 41 characters, which described that is silver was one of the presents which paid tribute to the Emperor Dezong Lishi by an offical Peishu who was the master of Yuezhou. According to the historical data, the time of paying tribute might be between Emperor Dezong 15th year of ZhengYuan (799A. D) and 19th year of Zhen Yuan (803A. D)

刻花鎏金鸞鳳紋銀盤
Gilt Silver Plate with Phoenix Design

皇后玉璽

西漢（公元前206—公元8年）

通高2cm，邊長2.8cm，重33克

1968年9月于陝西咸陽市出土

玉璽呈四方體。頂端"螭虎"作紐，虎作盤臥狀，首尾向左蜷曲。頭枕前爪，兩眼圓睜，開口露齒，雙耳貼首。印面為陰刻篆書"皇后之璽"，印體四面有綫刻雲紋。

此印為一小學生在狼家溝水渠邊無意中發現。秦始皇統一中國后，曾規定只有皇帝印章才稱"璽"，大臣以下稱"印"。據《漢官舊儀》載："皇后玉璽文與帝同。皇后之璽，金螭虎紐。"記載與此璽吻合。又據史書記載：西漢末年，赤眉農民起義攻入長安后，長陵被掘，便殿被焚。有可能玉璽于此時遺落土中，后被冲到長陵山腰的水溝里。現出土地點位于漢高祖劉邦和皇后呂雉合葬墓西側約一千米。從玉璽形制和出土地點判斷，很可能是呂后生前使用過的印鑒。

此璽通體晶瑩溫潤，系羊脂玉（即和田玉）。有光澤略顯透明，白色中夾雜有青、綠、黃、棕等色。此璽下方顏色較重，給人鈐印后未及揩拭的感覺，這是玉料雕琢時的匠心獨運。

玉璽印文排布疏朗，結體方整，筆畫勻稱，筆勢方中帶圓，剛柔相濟，刀法自然嫻熟，字體端正圓潤，與秦嶧山碑書法近似，是迄今所見唯一的一方古代皇后印璽。"文革"時期，江青曾傳令要調走此印，據為己有，由于各方巧妙抵制，未能得逞。

The Jade Seal of The Queen

The western Han Dynasty (206—B. C—8A. D)

H. 2cm, L. of each side 2.8cm W. 33g.

Unearthed at Xian yang City, Shaanxi, in Sep. 1968·

This is a cubic jade seal, On the top of the seal is a knobo of tiger. with its body prostrate, its head on the front claws, round eyes gogging and the ears stuck to the head. On the surface there is a four-character inscription inintaglio, "Huang Hou Zhi Xi", meaning the seal of the Queen, on the four sides, there are cloud designs carved in intaglio.

It was found by a student accidently by the ditch at longjia gou, after the first emperor of Qin unified China, stipulated that only the seal of emperor called Xi and the misister's seal called "yin" According to the historicaldata, recoded that the seal of the Queen had knob of tigar, which tallies with this seal. There was another recording, in the end of eastern Dynasty, the Red Brow restaurant upsing troops captured Changan, Chanliang mausoleum were digged, this seal might be fall down in the mud, them was washed into the ditch hear Changliang mauso-leum. The palace where unearthed the seal was 1000 meters to the Changliang. According to the shape of the seal and the place, which might be used by the Empress Lyehou.

The whole body of this seal is sparking and sleek, which is made of Hetian jade. This white jade is crystal and clear, there is green, yellow, brown, etc. in the white.

Thd style of its calligraphy is vigourous and graceful, the carving is smouth and natural, it is the magnificent jade seal of the Queen of ancient time.

皇后玉璽
The Jade Seal of the Queen

刻花白玉杯

唐 （公元618—907年）
高3.5cm，口徑5.5—10cm
1970年10月于陝西西安市
南郊何家村出土

刻花白玉杯呈八曲橢圓形，每曲似一蓮花瓣，組成一朵冰肌玉潔的蓮花，燦然開放。杯形似碗，杯身無耳，底有橢圓形圈足。玉杯為和田白玉，半透明狀。杯腹每曲刻有蔓草和花卉紋飾，以入刀較寬的斜陰綫刻劃而成，給人以淺浮雕效果。每曲紋飾獨立構圖，又渾為一體。

唐人喜歡飲酒，又喜愛蓮花。用玉器雕成飲酒器具，美酒入杯，或晶瑩剔透，或色如琥珀，可添詩情，可增雅興。唐代大詩人李白《客中行》曾吟咏道："蘭陵美酒鬱金香，玉碗盛來琥珀光。"就是對當時用玉制酒具飲酒的真實感受和喜悅心情的抒發。

刻花白玉杯瑩潤潔白，玲瓏可愛，紋飾素雅，內在和諧。雕工精巧，器壁很薄，花瓣棱綫分明，曲線流暢。它那種似凸實凹的表現手法，為唐代雕工的一個重要特徵，與漢代玉雕上的細若游絲的陰綫刻，已迥然不同。刻花白玉杯既有材質美，又具裝飾美，還有實用價值，是唐代風格玉器中的上乘之作。

White Jade Cup with Flower Design

Tang Dynasty（618*b*-907）
H・3.5cm，D・of mouth
5.5—10*cm*.
Uneathhed at Hejiacun，Xian City，In Oct. 1970.

This white jade is the octagonal oval in shape，each side like a lotus-peatl，which like a sparking and crystal-clear lotus，bright and shinning. The shape of the cup like a bowl，with out ear，under the bose is a oval ring foot，this cup is made of Hetian jade，each side of the belly，carved the flowers design in intaglio with wide lines，which like relief. Design on each side is unique and unified together as a whole pattern.

The people liked driking wine and loved totusi in the Tang Dynasty they carved the wine cup with jade when poured good wine into the jade cup，the colour of the wine and jade are crystal-clear and like amber. The great poet libai in the Tang Dynasty，who wrote a poem which describe that drinking wine with jade vessel was delightful exciting.

This jade cup is white and crystal-clear，exqusitely and design is elengant and simple. Carving is fine and perfect，the wall of the vessel is very thin，the arrises of the petals are clear and graceflul. The style of its carving is different from the fine carving in intaglio on the jade of Han Dynasty. This white joe cup has thee beatuty of material and decoration，and with value of practical，which is a master-piece of the jade vessels in the Tang Dynasty.

刻花白玉杯
White Jade Cup with Flower Design

鹿紋瓦當

春秋時代·秦（公元前770
年—前476年）

面徑14．4cm

1974年陝西鳳翔縣靳年宮
遺址出土

秦代瓦當多以動物圖形作
爲裝飾，鹿紋則是最有代表性
的一種。

此鹿紋占據整個瓦面。單
鹿昂首挺頸，作奔騰跳躍之狀，
刻劃得靈巧活潑，槪括生動。雖
然構圖受到空間的限制，由於
工匠抓住了奔鹿的形神特徵，
以簡練明快的造型，自然均衡
的布白，活現出一只機靈的奔
鹿形象。

秦漢之際的藝術作風，繼
承了戰國時代的傳統，進一步
擺脫了商周遺留下來的圖騰幽
靈，手法更趨于寫實。現實生活
中的動植物逐漸成爲藝術表現
的對象，同時也帶來了淸新喜
人的風格。鹿紋在名宮巨殿、離
宮別館等建築中多有表現。除
單鹿紋外，還有雙鹿紋、鹿魚
紋、鹿龜雁紋、鹿雁犬蟾蜍紋
等，那夸大的角、細長的頸、瘦
勁的腿，特點極爲突出。形象簡
潔靈活，極富動勢，表現力之強
使人嘆服。

鹿諧音"祿"，古人認爲是
富貴吉祥的象徵，故成爲秦時
瓦當的重要裝飾紋樣。鹿紋瓦
當的出土地鳳翔，古爲雍州，秦
的先公先王曾建都于此。這一
瓦當應是秦始皇統一六國前的
遺物。

Eave Tile with Deer Design

Qin Kindom of the Spring and Autumn Period.（770—476B. C）

D·14. cm.

Unearthed at the site of Qianan Place，Fengxiang county. Shaanxi in 1974.

Most of the eave liles were decorated with animals pattern in the Qin Dynasty，and deer design was one type which was popular.

The pattern of deer occupies the whole Lace of the tile，one deer is holding head high，in a posture of jumping，which is design simply and vivdly. As composition was limited by the space，the crasman caught the feature of the running deer，who used simple and lucid shape，expressing a smart life like running Deer.

The artistic style of Qin and Han Dynasty，carried forward the trddition of warring States period，got rid of the specture and totem left from Shang，Zhou Dynasties，which is tending to real. The real plant and animal became the objects of the arts，which brought new fresh style. Deer-design was popular at the royal place. Great hall，buildings. Beside lone deer pattern there were double-deer design，deer-fish design，deer-turtle design etc，the overstate horns，slenderneck，thin but sturdy legs，these features were very porjecting. The form is simple and artive，with graceful expression.

Deer has a homony which is "lu"，meaning of proper and huky，so deer pattern was popular design of the eave tiles in the Qin Dynasty. Unearthed in Fengxiang County. Where was the captial of early Qin. This eave tile should be the relic before Qinshihuang unified China.

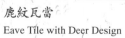

鹿紋瓦當

Eave Tile with Deer Design

夔鳳紋大瓦當

秦（公元前221—前207年）

通高48cm，面徑61cm

1977年于陝西臨潼縣清理秦始皇陵北建築遺址時出土

瓦當爲大半圓形，背有筒瓦殘長32cm。正面是一對高浮雕夔鳳紋，以鏡面對稱作左右排列，鳳身有陰刻細綫。夔鳳轉折盤曲布滿整個瓦當。

瓦當是古代建築檁頭筒瓦前端的遮檔，其作用是保護木椽不因日曬雨淋而朽爛，也有美化裝飾作用。夔鳳紋大瓦當是當今所發現存世最大的瓦當，被譽爲"瓦當王"。這個瓦當上的夔鳳紋經過精心構思，形象夸張，紋樣活躍，綫條遒勁，極富曲綫美和立體感。紋飾風格與商周青銅器一脈相承。其紋樣排布與空間布白構成瑰奇瑰麗的神秘氛圍，具有強烈的裝飾意趣。從此瓦當之大，可以想象出當時殿宇建築曾是何等宏偉龐大，它是我國古代建築材料少見的珍品。

秦始皇作爲"千古一帝"，在兼并六國、統一天下之后，即爲自己建造陵墓和陵園建築。這件夔鳳紋大瓦當正是他皇權思想的歷史見證，也爲我國建築史的輝煌提供了證據。

Big Cave Tile with phoenix Pattern

Qin Dynasty（221—207B·C）
H. 43cm, D. of face. 61cm.
Unearthed from Qishihuang's mausoleum at Lintong County, Shaanxi, in 1977.

This eave tile is semicirde in shape, on the back with a 32cm in length-tube tile. On the face there are two symmtrical high phoenix designs in relief, with fine lines carving in the patterns in intaglio. The designs are curling and occupy the whole face of eave tile.

Eave tile was used as the cover put on the head of the purlin of the building, which kept the rafter from the sun and rain, which also used for decoration. This eave tile is the biggest eave tile of the world up to know, call the King of eave tile. The phoenixs designs on it, the plot of it is elaborately designs, the form is pverstate, the patterns are active, the lines are graceful and vigorous. The style of the pattern isquite silimar with the patterns on the bronze wares of Shang and Zhou Dynasty, the patterns with the blank space form the mysterious atmosphere, according to its big size, we could image the grand hall and place at that time, which is a precious object of ancient building materials.

Being the first emperor of the feudal siciety, Qinshihuang had ordered the people built mausoleum for him after he unified Chins. This piece is proof of his aut hority thoughts and splendid Chinese architectural history.

夔鳳紋大瓦當
Big Cave Tile with Phoenix Pattern

四神瓦當

西漢（公元前206—公元8年）

面徑16—19cm，邊輪寬2—2.1cm

1956年西安漢長安城遺址出土

四神由來頗早。遠古時期，人們對許多自然現象不理解，以為有的動物能騰雲駕霧，呼風喚雨；有的動物勇猛異常，威鎮百獸；有的動物能翱翔天宇，按季往返；有的動物能通行水陸，長命百歲。心靈產生崇拜，部落奉為圖騰。商代，人們把天空四方的星象組成東方青龍、南方朱雀、西方白虎、北方玄武，以后作為方位或地域概念。到漢代，四神也被視為武力的象徵，并常出現在宮殿裝飾瓦當及銅鏡上。

瓦當是古代建築中，用來覆蓋屋頂坡面的灰陶片，瓦頭為圓形或半圓形。瓦當的裝飾形式，服從建築整體的要求；制作規格，配合建築規模的需要；圖象的風格，體現着統治者的意識。四神瓦當為單象畫面，均為模壓成型，當同一畫面同一方位橫向排列，既統一又莊嚴，具有實用和裝飾雙重價值。

龍紋瓦當，內飾青龍，張嘴彎頸，四足蹬開，其勢若奔。通體鱗甲，飛翼上卷，龍尾上翹，體態似虎，頭尾如龍。瓦當畫面清晰，邊緣殘損。整個造型渾厚飽滿，風格雄奇奔放，表現了龍的神秘和威嚴。

虎紋瓦當，內飾白虎，瞠目抵耳，張嘴若吼，白虎身驅圍繞中心圓，四腿伸展，勢若奮騰。虎身條紋班駁，虎尾屈升，布白均衡。整體造型動態優美，風格具象寫實，表現了虎的威武和雄健。特別是虎身條紋依動態用綫，自然流暢，再現了虎肌的彈性與質感。

朱雀瓦當，內飾朱雀，口銜寶珠，昂首翹尾，飛翼上舉，兩足奔走，通體羽毛，裝飾華貴。由於朱雀是鳳凰與飛禽綜合，由古人主觀臆想的吉祥之鳥，故形象浪漫，整體造型富於想象，風格典麗華美。特別是朱雀胸前尾下和翅翼上端，羽毛下垂曲卷，表現了朱雀飛起瞬間的動態，顯得靈動可愛。

玄武瓦當，內飾龜蛇，靈龜爬伏，騰蛇盤繞，形象怪異，神秘莫測。據專家研究，在上古神話中，玄武本名玄冥，是水神。玄冥是上古時少昊氏的理水之官。他為治水而死，后被尊為水神。水神本體是鯀，其象征是鱉。大禹之田叫修巳，修是蛇，鯀是鱉，龜蛇結合體形象是修（蛇）與鯀（鱉）夫婦的象徵性變型。玄武整體造型"綫""面"結合，圓中透方，風格緊湊中顯自然，凝重中見活潑，表現了玄武的玄妙和神異。

青龍、白虎、朱雀、玄武即表示東、西、南、北四個方位，又有驅邪除惡、鎮宅吉祥的含意，故盛行于漢代。從瓦當造型的考究，可以想象當時宮廷宅第的雄偉富麗，也體現出工匠們的高度智慧和藝術才情。

The Four Patron Saint Eave Tile

Western Han Dynasty (206—8A·D)

D. 16—19cm, width of edge 2—2.1cm.

Unearthed in 1956 at Ruins of Changan site of the Han Dynasty, Shaanxi.

The four patron sainte are of long standing. In remote antiquity, the people, made thethotem with seveal ancient design; In the Shang Dynasty, the people tormed the constellations on the four directions as wast-green dragon, south-white tiger, west-red scarlet bird, north-turtle, which defend the direstions and distrits later. In the Han Dynasty, the four saint symbolized the armed strength, then were decorated on the bronze mirrors and places.

The patterns on the eave tiles, according to the building the style of the pattterns, symbolized the thoughts of rulers.

Eave tile with dragon design, with a green dragon, opening its mouth and coiling the neck, in runing posture. There are scales on the body, wings are rolling upwards the tail sticking upward, the body like a tiger's, head and tail look like dragon's. The design on the tile is clear the edge is broken. The form is vogourous and graceful, the style is bold and flowing, shows the serious and mytherious expression of the dragon.

The eave tile withtiger design, decorated with a white tiger, eyes goggling, opening the mouthlike roaring, the body of its surrounding the central circle, four legs are streching, in a runing posture. The lines are carved finely in the·body, the tail is loiling and holding up. The form and posture are graceful and life like, style is realistic shows the strength and force, specially, the lines on its body are carved allow the posture, which are maturally showing the spring and real of the musle.

Eave tile with red scarlet, adorned with scarlet bird, holding apeal in its mouth, holding up the head and tail, wings are holding upwards, two feet are running, leathers of the body are decorated splendidly. Because the red soarlet bird unified the phoenix with bird it is a mythological bird, then the shape is romatic and full of imagination, the style is magnificent and elegant. Specially, the coiling leather on the wings under the chest shows the beauty of flying posture.

Eave tile with Xuan Wu, adorned with turtle and snake, the turtle is crawling, and the snake is coiling, the form is strange and mysterous According to the experts research, Xuan Wu originally named XuanMing which was the patrion saite of water, and from was unified snake and turtle. The whole shape of XuanWu is unified with "line" and face style is nature and graceful, shows the mysterious posture.

The green dragon, white tiger, red scarlet brid and Xuan Wu are called the four patron sainte mythologically, they defend the four directions: the east, west, south, and north. and also get rid of the ghosts. Guarding the residence luckily, so which were popular in the Han Dynasty. According to the elegant shape, we could imagine the splendour and magnificence of the palace, residence at that time, which mirror the wisdom and skill of the craftsman in the Han Dynasty.

四神瓦當
The Four Patron Saint Eave Tile

踞坐俑

秦（公元前221——前207年）

高 65cm

1976 年于陝西臨潼縣秦始皇陵園馬廄坑出土

這尊踞坐俑，絲絲細髮，分梳兩顯，螺形髮髻，挽于腦後。頭微前傾，雙目平視，嘴唇緊閉，神情嚴肅。雙膝着地踞坐，上身略微后仰，臀部置于腳跟。身穿交襟長衣，雙臂自然下垂，兩手半握拳頭，搭于雙膝之上。從面容身姿觀察，這是一位年輕純樸的養馬人形象。

踞坐俑造型準確，神態安詳。工匠精心雕刻，細部十分逼真。頭髮梳理整齊，胡須清晰可辨，衣紋走向自然，指甲一絲不苟。外形的細膩，更突現了坐俑溫順恭敬、認真負責的性格特徵，使人強烈地感受到這是一個經過精心挑選的忠于職守的養馬人。

據考古發現證明，古人席地而坐，就是踞坐姿勢。這種習俗從商代開始，一直保留到南北朝。唐代開始，才由踞坐逐步轉為盤腿而坐。踞坐俑的出土，提供了踞坐的真實形象。

Pottery Figure Kneeling and on Heel Sitting

Qin Dynasty (221—207B. C.)

H. 65cm.

Unearthed at the stable pit of the mausoleum of Qinshihuang, Lintong County, Shaanxi in 1976.

This figure, fine fair style is a cone in shape, which is coiled at the back of the head. The head extends forward a bit, two eyes watching flatly, lips closing, with serious expression. He sits kneeling on his heels, wears a over lapped lapels of garment, shoulders drooping naturally, wot handsin half fist shape putting on his knees. According to his face felling and posture, he is a young honest horse raiser.

The shape of this fogure is perfect, the manner is composed. The craftsman carved it very finely, the hair is tidy and moustache is clear to see, the run of the cloth veins is natural, the figure nails are fine. According to his expressionfrom the exquisite shape, he is an honest and faithful on horse raiser.

This sitting posture started from the Shang Dynasty, kept to the southern and northern Dynasty. The posture of sitting because became siting and coiling legs from this in the Tang Dynasty. This figure supplies real form of sitting on heels kneeling.

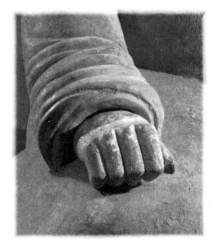

跽坐俑
Pottery Figure
Kneeling and on Heel Sitting

跪射武士俑

秦（公元前221—前207年）

高120cm

1974年于陕西临潼縣秦始皇陵二號坑出土

武士俑頭側束髮挽髻，用朱紅髮帶束扎髻根。眉骨微起，雙目平視，薄唇緊閉，棱角分明。身穿戰袍，外披鎧甲，右膝着地，左腿蹲曲，呈半跪射狀。足蹬方口齊頭鞋，雙手在身體右側作上下握弓狀。

此俑身材魁偉，相貌清俊，年輕英武，姿態矯健。工匠采用仿眞寫實的手法，對人物塑造一絲不苟：縷縷髮絲，梳理有序；甲片扎帶，環環相接；鎧甲甲釘，細致精微；髻上束帶，翻卷自如，給人細膩逼眞的強烈感受。而戰袍裙褲則又處理得自然明快。人物形象重在體現神武鷹揚的精神氣質和斗志昂揚的內心世界，并維妙維肖地表現出武士的沉着剛毅和機警敏捷的性格特征。同時，反映出工匠觀察的精細和刻劃入微。

跪射武士俑在二號坑戰斗方陣的東端，方陣全由弩兵組成。陣表爲站立式，陣心爲跪式，眞實地表現了當時的戰斗情景。古時射箭，每次三發，發射完畢，重新上箭。一立一跪，交替發射，彌補了裝箭的時差，便能達到萬箭齊發，矢如雨下。

Pottery Figure kneeling and Shooting

Qin Dynasty (221—207).

H. 120cm.

Unearthed in 1974 at the No. 2 pit of Qinshihuang's mausoleum.

Lint ong County, Shaanxi.

This figure with coiled hari on the top of his head, which is tied by a ribbon, his supe cillary ridge is up, eyes are watching foward lips closing tightly. He wears fighting robe, covered with atmour, the right leg kneeling and shooting on the earth, the left leg coiling, form knelling and shooting posture. Two hands make a shape of holding bow in the right side on the body.

This figure is young and brave, handsome and in vigourous posture The craftsman chosed the realistic meathod, carved every detail finly, hair, armour, ribbonetc. Which shows the character of the soilder and mirror, the high class skill on the carving of the craftsman at that time.

This figure is at the east side of the No, 2 pit, this square battle formation formed with arches. The a rches on the side are standing, in the central are kneeling. In ancient time, the archer was shooting with three arrows generally, after that got arrows again, one is standing and the other kneeling shooting alternately, which remedy the time of getting arrows and make the arrows like the rain.

跪射武士俑
Pottery Figure Kneeling and Shooting

彩繪騎馬俑

西漢（公元前206—公元8年）

通高68cm

1965年于陝西咸陽市楊家灣漢墓出土

楊家灣漢墓是漢高祖劉邦的陪葬墓之一，共出土騎兵俑583件，陶俑1965件，盾牌410件。陶俑作五列六行排列，前三列六坑為騎兵俑，后二列四坑為陶俑，有文官武士，也有樂舞雜役。

這件彩繪騎馬俑，騎者頭上有一圈顏色鮮亮的朱紅色繞過前額，兩鬢和后腦勺，為束斂頭發的"陌額"。兩目前視，神情專注。身穿鑲邊袍服，一手握繮繩，一手持器械。陶馬仰首張口露齒，鼻翼舒張，雙目突鼓，對天作嘶鳴狀。馬脖勁挺，馬身內收，馬臀渾圓，四足挺立，顯得驃肥體壯，雄健威武，造型壯美，神采飛揚。工匠着力刻劃了駿馬飽滿渾厚的體軀，體現出內在的勁力，給人以一往無前、銳不可擋的藝術感受。同時，也反映出當時的歷史眞實。

西漢時期，為了國防和交通要道的安全，騎兵成為重要的保衛勁旅。楊家灣出土的騎兵俑和步兵俑，形象地反映了以步、騎為主的軍陣場面。

Painted Pottery Figure Riding on House

Western Han Dynasty (179—141B)

H. 68cm.

Unearthed in 1965 at Yang jiawan, Xian yang city, Shaanxi.

Tomb at yangjiawan is the buried tomb fot the Emperor Liubang, from here, unearthed 583 pieces of figures on hores. 1965 pieces of pottery figures, 410 pieses of shields. The pottery figures are in 5 list and 6 lines, the back 2 lists in 4 pits are figures riding horses, the front 3 lists in 6 pit sare figures riding horses.

This figure, on the ride a head, there is a bright red circle which is round the forehead, the temples and the back head, called "moe" for holding hair. His two eyes are liking ahead carefully. He wears rob with inlaid the edge, one hand holding the reins, and the other handing the wvapon. The pottery horse opened mouth, two eyes are projecting, which is in posture of neighing to the sky. The four legs of the horse are standing steady, the neck is vigourous and show the expression of strong and forceful. The craftsman formed the horse in a vigourous body and strong posture mirroring the real of the history.

In the Western Han Dynasty, in order to keep the traffic road, cavalry became the important troop which was on duty. The warriors and horses unearthed at Yangjiacun, which show the combination of the eavalry and infantryman.

彩繪騎馬俑
Painted Pottery Figure Riding on Horse

大喇叭裙女立俑

西漢（公元前206—公元8年）

高31cm

西安市漢長安城遺址出土

此俑頭戴風帽，身穿長袖交襟束腰長裙。雙手前拱，置于腰際。兩袖寬鬆，多條皺褶匯聚胸側；長裙下曳，裙擺鋪成大喇叭狀。

這件女立俑儀態端莊，比例勻稱，綫條流暢，手法凝煉。工匠塑造人物，注重取大勢，去繁縟，追求整體效果。即不求形體的逼真和細節的雕琢，而只求總體上把握表現對象的神韵，賦予其端麗嫻淑的氣質。人物面部刻劃簡約，卻明明透露出清純恬靜的風韵。衣袖的平滑皺褶表現了柔軟的絲綢質感。纖細的腰肢和展開的長裙，襯托出亭亭玉立的婀娜身姿。在賦予纖纖細腰表現人物輕盈柔美之時，又以寬大鋪開的裙擺強調人物的曲綫美。這種誇張的造型手法，既克服了單純強調"瘦"帶來的纖弱之嫌，又增加了女立俑的穩定感，使總的格調顯現為含蓄內向。這是西漢女俑中一件罕見的佳作。

Flared Skirt Female Standing Figure

Western Han Dynasty (206—8A. D.)

H. 31cm.

Unearthed in the remains of Changan in the Han Dynasty. Xian City.

This figure wears a bowl-like hat, with a broad-sleeved interback lapes skirt tied round her waist. Her two hands are cupping in front of her waist. Two sleeves are wide and loose, with much fine and close wovenfolds gathering at the breast. The long skirt drooping down, and the lower part of skirt spreading like a flared bell.

The shape of this figure is finr, its lines smooth, proportipned, harm nious, the workmanship, sccint and brief, perfectly expressing the inner world of this figure. She looks pretty, with an air of the inner world of this figure. She looks pretty, with an air of reservedness and elegance. The folds reflects the softness of the quality of material. Slender waist and limbs and the great spreading skirt, sets off the figures and graceful posture.

The overstate forming method, which overcome the shortcoming of emphasizing the slim, also raising the firm of the standing fiure. This is a precious rare masterpiece of female figures in the Western Han Dynasty.

大喇叭裙女立俑
Flared Skirt Female Standing Figure

彩繪跽坐俑

西漢（公元前206—公元8年）

高33cm

1966年7月于陝西西安市東郊任家坡出土

此俑秀髮熨貼，中分兩顯，披至頸后，束爲垂髻。面容平和，眉清目秀，鼻若懸膽，雙唇緊眠。身穿三重衣，外衣爲褐色長襦，內衣淺紅，曲領高厚。雙膝幷攏着地，兩手抱于腹際，直體端坐，臀部壓在腳掌上，呈恭敬服從的跽坐姿勢。

這件俑出土在西漢孝文帝竇太后陵的從葬坑里，同坑出土立式或坐式陶俑42件。陶質堅實色靑，扣之鏗然有聲。其造型質樸寫實，比例勻稱，體態端莊，衣着形制和色澤如實模擬，再現了漢代婦女的品貌和裝束。

從藝術風格上看，工匠抓住對象的本質特征，用圓渾的手法對人物形體做粗輪廓的勾劃，而追求簡樸、內向、含蓄和渾然一體的藝術格調，力圖體現和傳達對象的內在精神和活力，喚起人們對雕塑形象眞實可親的耐人尋味的感覺，同時，給表現對象以人格美和崇高美的審美評價。

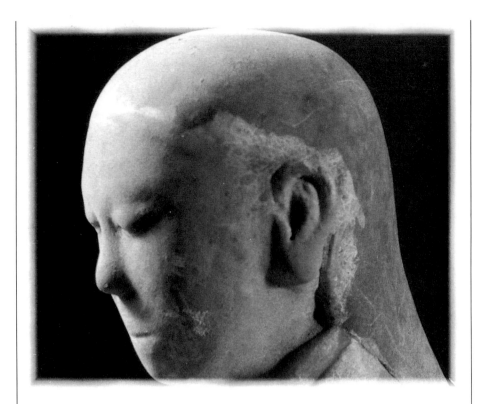

Painted Pottery Female Figur Sitting on Heels

Western Han Dynasty (206—8A. D.)

H. 33cm

Unearthed at Kenjiapo, east suburb of Xian City in 1966.

This female figure with drooping long hair style, which is devided in the contral top of her head. The expression of face is silent, pretty eyes and brows, lips closing tightly. She is wearing three clothes the outer is brown robe, the inner is light red, the coiling collar is high and thick. Double knees are closed and kneeling, two hands crossing by the belly, body is in a stight posture the buttocks on the heels, she is in a posture of sitting on heels respectfully.

It was unearthed from the tombs buried for the Quees Dou mausoleu of Emperor Xiaowen in the Weste Han Dynasty, unearthed 42 pieces pottery figures (indefferent) posture from here. The coulour of this figure is perfect and it is hard. The shape is brief and realistic proport ioned, posture is dignified, the style and colour of the cloth mirror the feature of the garment of the women in Han Dynasty.

According to the artistic style, the craftsman caught the characte of the object, made it with graceful and brief line, shows the inner world of the figure by the realistic form, the expression of gentel and lind in our sight.

彩繪跽坐俑
Painted Pottery Female Figure Sitting on Heels

彩繪文吏俑

西魏（公元535—556年）

高40cm

1977年于陝西漢中市崔家營西魏墓出土

文吏陶俑頭飾頂花，"魋髻"平指，橫長約五厘米。面龐嬌好，眉目清秀，五官端正，嘴含微笑。身穿右衽寬袖直領上衣，右臂下垂，袖長掩手；左臂平抬握拳，似持物件。下着寬筒裙褲，褲□袖□，俱呈寬□大喇叭狀，雙腳八字站立。

此俑造型褒衣博帶，苗條修長，秀骨清象，瀟灑倜儻。所穿服飾與同時的北魏俑風格迥異，為"蜀"、"滇"形象。特別頭飾"魋髻"，是蜀人習俗，表現出南北朝時代濃厚的地方色彩和民族融合的特徵。

Painted Pottery Figure of Civil official

Western Wei (535—556A. D.)

H. 40cm

Unearthed at tomb of western Wei at Caijiaying, Hanzhong City, Shaanxi in 1977.

This figure has a decoration on his head, which is about 5cm in length. His face is handsome, bright eyes, has regular features and with smiling. He wears a coat with wide sleeves and stright collar, drooping right arm, the sleeve is longer that right hand; the left arm is lifting up and holding a fist, which like holding something. He wears a wide flared trousers, standing in " 八 " form.

This figure's form is vigourous and graceful, slender

and handsom. The garment is quite different from the figure's of Northern Wei, which is the style of "Shu". "Dian". The special decoration on the head, was custom of people in Shu, shows the local style in the southern and northern Dynasties and the features of the mixing of nationalities.

彩繪文吏俑
Painted Pottery Figure of Civil Official

彩繪偏髻女立俑

唐天寶七年（公元748年）
通高54cm
1955年于陝西西安市高樓村出土

　　此俑頭梳偏髻，面龐豐潤，右臂彎于胸前，左臂自然下垂，體態肥腴，風韵高雅。身着V領窄袖寬袍，衣紋隨體型交于兩足之間，簡練明快，自然流暢，生動地表現了絲綢的質感。從殘留的色澤可以看出，原是朱紅長袍，上有天藍花紋。

　　女立俑是盛唐婦女審美時尚的生動反映。該俑墓主是唐玄宗時羽林軍長史吳守忠，死于天寶七年，年65歲。墓內幾乎全是陶俑，女俑多爲大髻寬衣，豐頰腴體。這和唐詩所描述的"風流薄梳妝，時世寬裝束"相印證。據說，唐玄宗寵愛的楊貴妃"天生麗質"，體態豐滿，肌膚白皙如"凝脂"，是一代美人的典型，因而，上有所好，下有所崇，以胖爲美遂成爲時代風尚。女主俑蕭灑的儀態姿容，既反映了盛唐社會貴婦養尊處優的歷史事實，又體現出她們嫻雅矜持的精神與風度，使藝術形象美與意境美比較完美地結合在一起。

Painted Pottery Female Standing Figure

Tianbao 3th year of Tang Dynasty （748A. D）
H. 54cm
Unearthed in 1955 at Gaolouan, Xian City, Shaanxi.

　　This female figure, he hair worned in bun on one side of the head, her face is plump and smooth-skinned, the right arm bending in front of the chest, the left arm drooping natually, her carriage is plentiful with elengant fraceful bearing. She wears a rose robe with "V" collar and narrow sleeves, the folds of garment follow the body and crissscross between two fect, naturally and gracefully, which shows the softness of the silk. According to the remaining colour, It's red robe with blue designs originally.

　　This figure is a life mirror of fanshional appreciation of beauy in the Tang Dynasty. It was unearthed from the tomb of Wusa Zhong, who was the general of the roual force in the time of Emperor XuanZong, who died in 7th year of Tianbao, and 75years old. The female figures unearthed from his tomb, mostly are big hair bun and plentiful. And the emperor of XuanZong's doted on a plentiful imperial concubine Yang, so from the time, which was fashionable of considering the fat as beauty. This figure reflects the real of noble women who enjoyed high position and lived in ease and comfort in the flourishing Tang Dynasty, and also mirror their reserved and elegant manner.

彩繪偏髻女立俑
Painted Pottery Female Standing Figure

彩繪黑人男立俑（2件）

唐大中四年（850年）

通高14．7cm—15cm

1948年于陝西長安縣嘉里村裴氏小娘子墓出土

此二俑爲非洲黑人形象。膚色黧黑，頭髮卷曲，眉骨突起，嘴唇厚闊。一俑身穿交襟長袍，衣袖上寬下窄，袍下擺提起系于腰間，兩臂下垂，緊握雙拳；一俑上身裸露，聳肩凸腹，雙目圓睜，眼白如燭，胸肌隆起，下著短褲，左臂下垂，右手捧腹，雙腿外叉，赤足着地，身體壯實，精悍有力。

二俑造型生動，形象逼眞，作者抓住了黑人的外型特征，刻劃出豪爽質樸的性格。二俑的出土，說明大唐對外開放，不僅通過絲綢之路加強了與中亞西亞和歐洲國家的聯系，影響還波及非洲。彩繪黑人男立俑正是中國和非洲人民友好往來的實物見證。

墓主裴氏小娘子，小字太，是裴均的孫女。裴均是庚高宗時期裴行儉的后人。裴行儉兼有文武才能，曾任禮部尚書兼檢校右衛大將軍，曾率軍30余萬討伐突厥，大破突厥于黑山。

Painted Pottery Standing Negro Figures（2 pieces）

In the 4th year of DaZhong of the Tang Dynasty（850A·D）

H·14．7—15cm.

Unearthed in concubine Pei's tomb in Changan County, Shaanxi 1948.

These figures are Afria negro froms. They are black skin, with curled hair, projecting supercilliary ridges, thick lips. One of them wears an interlaced lapels, a long robe with its aleeves and wide in the upper part and narrower in the lower part, his arms hanging down and fist clenched. The other figure exposes his upper part of the body（shur gging）the shoulders, bulging his belly, his muscle of chest getting prominet, the right hand holding his belly, his left arm hangs down, legs stepped apart, with his feet bare, his body is strong and vigorous.

These figures were portraged life-like, the craftsman firmly grasping the Black's facial figure features, who caught the vivacity of the Black, reflect the forthright and unadorned characteristics of the negroes. These figures, proved that after opening external in the Tang Dynasty, China strengthed the relations with the countries of Mid-asia, Western-asia and Europe by the silk road, which also influenced the Africa. The two figures are the witness of the contracts and friendship between the chinese people and the people in Africa.

The master of the tomb was Pei's concubine, who named Tai, was the granddaught of Peijun.

彩繪黑人男立俑
Painted Pottery Standing Negro Figures

彩繪説唱俑（一組三俑）

唐（公元618—907年）

高18—23cm

1966年于陕西西安市西郊工地出土

這組説唱俑有説唱者一人，伴奏者二人。説唱者高23cm，為一長鬚長者，坐于圓拱形繡墩上，頭戴幞頭，身穿圓領長袍，仰首向天，雙目微合，正沉浸在説唱情景中。一樂俑盤腿坐在圓形蒲團上，雙手握笙，正在吹奏；一樂俑則兩腿交叉，側身而坐，正在彈撥樂器。表情專注傳神，仿佛陶醉于表演之中。

中國説唱藝術與絲綢之路密切相關。公元1世紀，佛教東傳，一種邊講邊唱宣講佛經的形式"講唱"隨之傳入。后逐漸適應本土風情，僧侶們采用民間流行題材和曲調傳播佛理，由"經變"到"俗變"，到開元、天寶時的"變場"，形成中國風格的説唱藝術形式。這組説唱俑造型形象生動，情景交融，是中國説唱藝術盛行于唐代的物證。

Painted Pottery Figures in Performance（a proup with 3 pieces）

Tang Dynasty（618—907A·D）

H. 18—23cm.

Unearthed in 1966 at West suburb of Xian City, Shaanxi.

This group has a figure in talking and singing, two figures inaccompanying. The figure in talking and singing is 23cm in height, who is an old man with long beard, sitting on a round arched garden stool, with a scarf wraped his hair, wearing a long robe with round collar, holding head high and facing sky, closing eyes, who is immersed in talking and singing. One figure is coiling legs and sitting on a rush cushion, two handsholding a sheng (a reed pipe wind instrument) and playing; the other figure is crossing two legs and sitting with an angle, who is playing the instrument. They are all attention as if revel in performing.

The art of talking and singing is connected with the silk road. 1st century A. D. the buddism was propagated into China, so did the style of talking and singing inexplainging the buddist sutra. Later, the monks propagated the buddist sutra with popular themeand rythem among the people, changed the style of talking and singing. Up to the reign of Tian bao, Kaiyuan, in the Tang Dynasty, formed the chinese style art of talking and singing. There figures are made life-like, which are witness of the art in talking and singing being popular in the flourishing in the Tang Dynasty.

彩繪説唱俑
Painted Pottery Figures in Performance

雙環望仙髻女俑

唐高宗永徽三年（公元652年）

高58.2cm

1983年7月于陝西西安市棗園村東唐墓出土

此俑面如滿月，寬額豐頤，修眉細目，櫻桃小口，頭梳雙環望仙髻。身穿寬袖羅襦，足蹬雲頭花履。頭部偏側，肚腹挺起，臂披長巾，長裙曳地。兩手舉于胸前，手中好似持物。

女俑出自唐特進右衛大將軍雁門郡開國公俾失十囊的墓葬。俾失十囊，字自牧，西突厥族，陰山人，于唐太宗開元初臣服于唐，唐高宗永徽三年（公元652年）死于禮泉縣。墓中共出土陶俑57件，雙環望仙髻女俑僅此一件。

從女俑造型看，嬌生慣養，雍容疏懶，一派養尊處優者的形象。她那華麗時髦的打扮裝束，百無聊賴的神情氣質，故作嬌憨的神態舉止，生動地刻劃出一個飽食終日、無所用心的富貴女子的身姿。她外表的華貴與內心的空虛形成強烈的反差，成為個性鮮明、形神獨特的唐代女俑形象，顯示出工匠熟練的造型能力和個性化的表現方法，是一件耐人尋味的唐代雕塑藝術作品。

Pottery Female Figure

Tang Dynasty （618—907A. D.）

H. 58. 2cm.

Unearthed from the tomb or Tang Dynasty Zaoyuan cun, Xian City, Ahaanxi inJuly 1983.

This figure is smooth-skinned, Wide forehead and plentiful face with long eyebrows and delicate eyes, small mouth like a cherry, the hair is dressing in two round buns. The head is slanting, bulging belly, covering a long scarf onher shoulder, the long skirt is spreading on the earth. Her two hands are lifting in front of her chest as if holding smething.

This figure was unearthed froma tomb of a general in the Tang Dynasty, who was a west Tujue, born in Yinshan, submitted himself to the rules of the Emperor Tai Zong in the Tang Dynasty, died in 3rd year of Yonghui of Emperor Gaozong （652A. D） at Liquan county. From his tomb, unearthed 57 pieces figures, this is the only one female figure like this.

This figure reflects a noblewoman who lived in clover and was wearing in fashionable style, and did nothing. There is astriking contrast between her splemdid experience and spiritual ballast, which is a uique female in the Tang Dynasty, and it is a masterpiece which affords much food for thought.

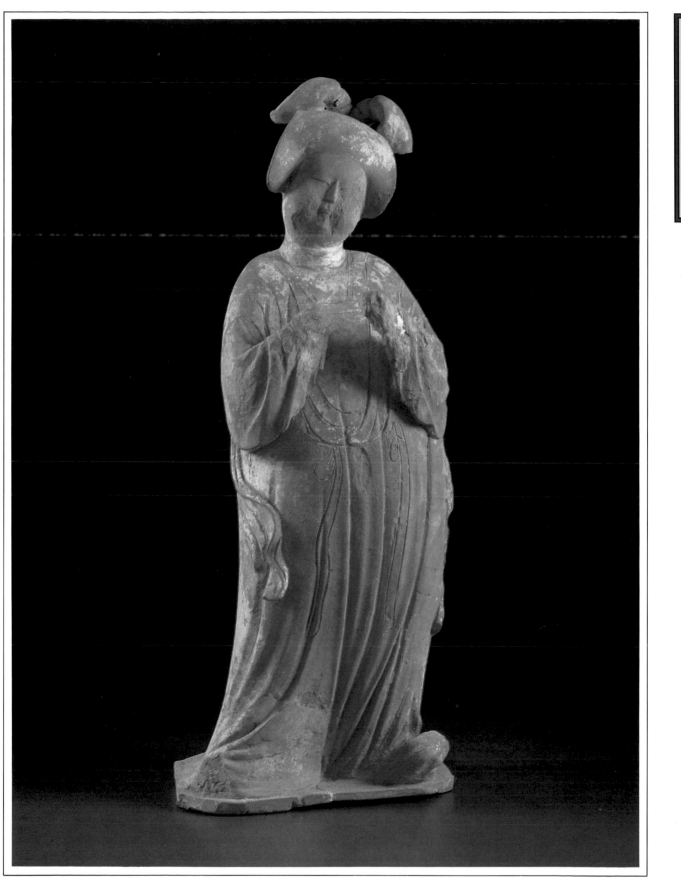

雙環望仙髻女俑
Pottery Female Figure

彩繪釉陶女騎俑

唐高宗龍朔三年（公元663年）

通高37cm，長29cm

1971年於陝西禮泉縣昭陵鄭仁泰墓出土

紅斑黃馬上，端坐着一位妙齡少女。她頭戴黑色涼帽，秀發裹着黑色紗巾，身着窄袖白衫，錦花袖頭，外套紅花短襦，腰系淡黃色條紋長裙，足穿黑色尖靴。左手緊勒馬繮，右手自然下垂。少女眉清目秀，櫻桃小口，面部豐潤，神態自若，端麗嫻靜。馬首下彎，張口似鳴，馬鬃梳理整齊，與馬唇和四蹄俱施朱紅，配以繡花座墊，顯得十分華貴，是一件寫實性很強的唐代彩塑，表現了唐代上層婦女的地位和時尚，也反映出域外文化的極大影響。

墓主鄭仁泰，名廣（601年—663年），17歲時追隨李世民父子起兵太原，勇敢善戰，后位至大將軍，列上柱國，封同安郡公。62歲去世，陪葬昭陵。彩繪釉陶女騎俑出土時，位於墓道小龕內群俑的最前列，說明身份不同尋常。

Painted Glazed Pottery Female Figure on Horse

In the third year of Long shuo of the Tang Dynasty (663A·D·)

H·37cm, L·29cm.

Unearthed in Zhong Rental's tomb at Liquan County. Shaanxi in 1971.

On the horse yellow glazed, dotted and dyed by red colour, a pretty young girl is sitting. On her hand is a blacksunshade hat, pretty hair wrapped with a silk-scarf, wearing a white long shirt with narrow sleeves, on which is added a red flowered jacket, a light yellow long skirt is tied in her waist, with a pair of black tapering shoes. Her left hands is pulling the halter, right hands drooping natrually. Her face looks round and fall with bright eyes and clear-eye-brows, red mouth like a cherry, she is pretty gentle and refined. The horse turned down the head, opening mouth like reigh, with tidy mane, its lips and hoofs are glazed with red, with a emborider chshion on the saddle, shows splendour, this is a realistic painted pottery of Tang Dynasty, which reflects the fashion and status of the noble woman of the Tang Dynasty, and mirrors the influence by the culture abroad.

The master of the tomb was Zhengrentai, named Guang (601—663A. D.) who was a famous brave general, died when he was 63years old, and buried in mausoleun. When this figure unearthed, it was in front of the group of pottery figures inside the tomb passage, which reflected her special status.

彩繪釉陶女騎俑
Painted Glazed Pottery Female Figure on Horse

彩繪釉陶文官俑

唐高宗龍朔三年(公元663元)

通高69cm

1971年陝西醴泉縣鄭仁泰墓出土

此俑頭戴深藍色梁冠，金飾冠頂。身著朱色寬袖長衫，青綠衣襟，腰束寬帶，袖裙和前胸均有彩色花飾。下裳為乳白寬松長褲，足蹬黑色如意高履。

文吏俑濃眉大耳，雙目炯炯，虯髯上翹，雙唇如丹，兩手合抱拱立，神情安詳肅然。工匠成功地抓住了宮庭仕官的職業特點，外型上刻劃其峨冠博帶、衣著華麗的形象，顯示其身份的高貴和地位的顯赫，而著重從面容和拱立姿態上賦予其道貌岸然、胸有城府的內在氣質，給人聰明睿智、神秘莫測的印象。他的服飾也是研究唐代宮廷官員品級和形制的珍貴實物資料。

Painted Glaze Pottery Figure of Civil Offical

In the 3rd year of Long-shuo of the emperor Guao Zong (663A. D.) of the Tang Dynasty.

Unearthed in the tomb of Zheng Rentai's at liquan county, Shaanxi. This figure wears a blue lofty hat, adorned with gold colour on its top. He wears a broad-sleeved red long garment, with dark green front part of it, tied a wide ribbon at waist, the collar and chest of which are adorned with coloured flower designs. He has on a pair of white loose trousers, cladding a pair of black "S" -shaped shoes.

He has big ears, wide-eyebrows and bright eyes, moustache is upward, red lips, he cups his two handson the chest, with a dignified and stately expression. The craftsman caught the features of the civil official, successfully portrayed on official with lofty hat and gorgeous dress, reflects his illustrious status, which shows the expression of wisdom and mysterious colours from his face and posture. And his uniforms provide us with materials for studing the uniforms of officials and systems of the offical in the Tang Dynasty.

彩繪釉陶文官俑
Painted Glaze Pottery Figure of Civil Officer

彩繪釉陶武官俑

唐高宗龍朔三年（公元663年）

通高72cm

1971年陝西禮泉縣昭陵鄭仁泰墓出土

武官俑胎質潔白堅硬，全身戎裝。頭戴胄幘，金飾胄頂，朱色幘巾。身著明鎧綠甲，雙臂飾獸面吞口。腰束寬帶，下着戰裙，足蹬皮靴。通身彩繪貼金，色彩絢麗斑爛。武官眉峰高聳，雙目圓瞪，鼻準隆起，雙唇緊閉，虬髯上翹，壯碩強悍。右臂前屈，左臂下垂，雙拳半握。雙腿叉開，足尖外張，偉岸挺拔，穩若磐石。整個造型神采英武，威風凛凛，活脫脫一副唐代武將的形象。

鄭仁泰墓出土的彩繪釉陶系高嶺土做坯，胎質白色，是唐三彩發展的前身。彩繪釉陶是雕塑藝術和繪畫藝術相結合的佳作，為研究唐三彩的發展過程提供了重要資料。

Painted Glazed Pottery Figure of Military Officer

In the 3rd year of Longshuo in the Tang Dynasety (663A. D.)

H·72cm.

Unearthed in Zheng Rentai's tomb at Liquan County, Shaanxi in 1971.

The rough cast of this figure is white and solid, he wears a golden scarf. He has on a suit of green armour, on the shoulder, adorned with animal-face, patterns, wearing a belt around his waist, with a long apron below, wearing a pair of leather shoes. The whole body is colour-painted and filled with gold leafs, which looks gorgeous and magnificent He has lofty brows, round stared eyes, the moustache sticking up. with strong and vigourous body. The logs stepped apartly and toes streched out, he stands upright, robust and tall, standing as firm as millstone. The figure is brave and majestic-looking, as a life-like general of the Tang Dynasty.

The figures unearthed from ZhengRentai's tomb, the rough casts were made of Kaolin and are white, which are the earlier state of the tri-coloured glazed pottery of Tang Dynasty. The painted and glazed pottery figures, are masterpiece which unified the sculpture and painting, which provide important materials of reaching the developing of the tri-coloured glazed pottery of the Tang Dynasty.

彩繪釉陶武官俑
Painted Glazed Pottery Figure of Military Officer

雙環髻舞女俑

初唐

通高37．8cm

1986年于陕西長武縣唐墓
出土

　　舞女俑頭飾雙環髻，臉如
滿月，眉目清秀，脖頸頎長，上
系項練。身穿圓領短袖尖齒裙，
肩垂帔帛，外套半臂，內穿窄袖
廣口紅條紋拖地長裙，腰束寬
帶，足蹬雲頭履。雙手置于胸
前，拇指食指朝上，其余三指作
半握拳，呈手捧蓮花狀。人物身
材苗條，神情虔誠，宛如"曹衣
出水"，端莊秀麗，輕盈婀娜。特
別是下垂的廣袖和罩住腳面的
小喇叭裙口，與仍在翻動似的
柳葉狀寬邊飾，相得益彰，恰似
正待起舞的一剎那默立，又似
曲終收舞的一剎那靜止，舞女
卻仍沉浸在裊裊余音的旋律和
意境中，給人無盡的美感享受。

　　這件彩繪雙環髻舞女俑造
型清麗，比例勻稱，靜中有動，
人物傳神，是初唐時期一件精
妙的寫實性塑像，其體態神貌
與敦煌壁畫的初唐女供養人畫
像，有某種异曲同工之妙。

Pottery Female Figure in Dancing and with Double-ring Buns

early Tang Dynasty.

H·37．8cm.

Unearthed in Changwu County, Shaanxi in 1986.

The hair of this figure dressed in double-ring buns. Her face is full and smooth-skinned, with delicate eyebrows and pretty eyes, long neck on which is a necklace, she wears lip-edged skirt with short sleeved and round collar, silkscarf to the earth with narrow sleeves but flared mouth, tying a wide ribbon around the wasist, with a pair of cloud-tip shoes, Two hands put before the chest, with holding up the thumbs and index figures, the others clenching in fist, as if holding a lotus. She is slim and refined. The drooping flared sleeves and the flared skirt with the willow-leaf-shaped decoration edge, reflect that silence before dancing girl is still immersed in the sweet rythem, shows endless enjoyment of beauty.

This figure is pretty and fresh, proportioned, there is silent within the moving, which is life-like, it is a perfect sulpture of early Tang Dynasty, which is quite similar with the female painting of frescos in Dunhuang.

雙環髻舞女俑
Pottery Female Figure in
Dancing and with Double-ring Buns

白陶誕馬

唐顯慶二年（657年）
通高46．5cm，長54cm
1972年於陝西禮泉縣唐張
士貴墓出土

誕馬，是跟隨儀仗備用的散馬。此馬通體純白如象牙雕刻，體格壯碩，造型逼真。三腿着地，右前蹄奮起。馬首低昂，雙耳直立，作嘶鳴狀。馬鬃梳理整齊，成十四絡波浪狀排列，馬尾縮起，尾部上揚。胸肌突怒，臀部渾圓，給人精神抖擻，威武雄壯的強烈印象。特別馬鬃的裝飾獨具特色，與毛色純淨的形體形成強烈的對比，增加了此馬的華美和高貴。誕馬的形象，與唐詩描寫的"君看此馬不受羈，天驕勢欲凌雲飛"兩相吻合。

墓主張士貴（586—657年）是隋末群雄蜂起的風雲人物之一。隨大業十三年（617年）歸附李唐父子。后屢立戰功，官至左領軍大將軍，封號國公。顯慶二年病亡，陪葬昭陵。

White Pottery Horse

In the 2nd year of Xian Qing of the Tang Dynasty (657A. D)

H. 46.5cm, L. 54cm.

Unearthed in Zhangshi gui's tomb at Li quan County, Shaanxi in 1972.

Dan horse was prepared for the ceremony and free horse. The whole horse is purely white as ivory carving, with a strong and robust body, the shape is life-like. Three legs stand on the ground, while the right front hoofs is lifting up. Its head is turning down, ears prick in neighing posture. The horse's mane is tidy, in 14 skein waves, the tail is coiled and raises. The muscle is prominent and the buttock is round, make the horse vigorous and strong. The unique bent horse's mane adds splendour and magnificent to this horse.

The master of this tomb, Zhangshigui was a famous person at the end of the sui Dynasty. In the 13th of Daye (617A. D.) he was obeyed the Emperor of Tang Dynasty, later he rendered services time and again, then was offered as Guoguo Minster. He died in 2nd year of Xianqing, was buried beside Zhaoling Mausoleum.

白陶誕馬
White Pottery Horse

跨馬彎弓射雕俑

唐（公元618—907年）

通高36.2cm，長30cm

1971年於陝西乾縣懿德太子李重潤墓出土

陶馬佇立，馬首微屈，兩耳仄立，鬃毛中分，梳理於前額兩側，整齊下垂，張嘴作奔跑暫停狀，馬尾縮起。一騎手頭紮幞頭，身穿圓領長衫，腰挎寶劍，側身仰望，注視着天空中的獵物，兩手若拈弓搭箭姿態。其神情正如唐詩描繪的那樣："半酣呼鷹出遠郊，弓彎滿月不虛發"。工匠抓住射手屏息射箭的瞬間，雖靜猶動，給人以百發百中的聯想，使造型意氣風發，栩栩如生。

這是一件反映唐室宮庭狩獵活動的陶俑。唐代，皇室宗親盛行狩獵活動，既可使弓馬不廢，強健體魄，又可怡情娛樂。當時，在唐長安城北大明宮以西，有專供皇帝貴戚狩獵娛樂的皇家禁苑和獵場。

跨馬彎弓射雕俑是一件仿絞胎工藝。絞胎是用白、褐色兩種色調的瓷土揉和拉坯，胎上出現變化多端的紋理，上釉焙燒而成。此俑仿絞胎效果，繪出紋理。馬臀紋理成豎長條，似突峭的峰巒；馬胸紋理，外粗內細，似圓又方，若急湍的漩渦。

所描紋理，綫條流暢，如行雲流水，使俑顯得絢爛錦綉。

這件射雕俑器胎純白，外繪紋飾，涂以釉色。是至今所能見到的造型精美的一件仿絞胎作品。

Pottery Figure Riding and Shooting With Bow

Tang Dynasty （618—907A.D.）

H. 36.2cm，L. 30cm.

Unearthed in 1971 at the tomb of crown price Yide, Li-chongrun，Qian xian County，Shaanxi.

The horse stands still，its head bents a little，the ears stand，the horse's mane is devided in the center which is combed tidy and drooping，opening the mouth is a rest after running，its tail is coiled. A rider on the horse，hair covered with a scarf on the head，wearing a long cape with round collar，carring a sword on the waist's belt，turning the body and looking up at the vulture in the sky，the two hands are in a posture of holding the bow and arrow. The craftsman caught the twinkling of shooting shows the image of every shot wits the target，and made the figure life like.

This figure is a mirroir of royal hunting in the Tang Dynasty. In the Tang Dynasty，hunting was popular in the royal families，it could keep the horse hunting and strengthen body，it was aslo a kind entertainmetr. At that time，there are royal form of hunting for the emperor and imperial families at the west of Daming Palace.

This is a piece of crafts imitating "Jiaotai". "Jiaotai" is the clay mixed with white，brown pigments was kneaded into semifinished products，after burn it in the kiln，the glaze is put on and burnt for second time through burning now the art effect，various veins appeared various veins appeared beneath the glaze. This figure imated that，paiting the veins. The vertical veins on the buttock like hills; the veins on the veins chest，thick and thin like the whirl. These veins are graceful and perfect，make the figure splendid and full of colour.

The roughcast of this figure is white，painting veins，then put on glaze and burnt，This is the only perfect piece of imatlting "Jiaotai"

跨馬彎弓射雕俑
Pottery Figure Riding and Shooting with Bow

白瓷胡人頭像

唐乾封二年（公元667年）

高16.5cm

1956年於陝西西安市韓森寨段伯陽墓出土

這個白瓷胡人頭，頭戴翻沿胡帽，帽沿飾排列有序的曲線表示胡帽為皮毛制品。帽沿罩住額頭，幾與眉毛相接。眉骨突起，呈半圓弧形，眉毛清晰刻出。雙眼圓睜，上眼瞼也突起，呈弧形。眼球凸出，用黑色點染，眼白也用綫勾出。高鼻由眉心和雙目間隆起，鼻翼舒張，面部肌肉上收鼓出，兩絡胡須隨鼓出的面頰蜿轉卷曲。兩唇微啟，唇綫下彎，似笑非笑，神情入微。腮部和下巴圍一圈濃密的絡腮胡，也由整齊的彎曲綫組成。整個面部刻畫精細，比例正確，人物表情詼諧有趣，給人憨直純樸的印象。釉色白中泛青，釉面有細碎開片。胎骨堅實致密，胎體上曾先施一層潔白的化妝土，再罩以透明的玻璃釉。這是唐代初期制瓷工藝和雕塑藝術完美結合的一件代表作。

與白瓷胡人頭像同一墓葬出土的還有：器形為西域少年形象的白瓷人形尊和白瓷貼花高足鉢，都是造型優美的藝術品。

White Porcelain Figure of Hu's Head

In the 2nd year of Qian feng of the Tang Dynasty (667A. D.)

H. 16.5cm.

Unearthed in Duanboyang's tomb at Hansenzai, Xian City, in 1956.

This head of a Hu (non-Han nationalities in ancient China) is white poecelain, with a rolling edged hat of "hu". On the edge adorned with curves shows it is a leather hat. The edge of the hat corved the forehead, closing to the eye-brows. The bone of eye-brow is raised and in arched, eye-brows are carved linely and clearly. Two eyes are gogging, the upper eyelids raising in arc. the eyeballs are protruding, glazed with black, and the white of the eyes painted with lines. The high nose is protruding between two eyes. opening the nostrils, the mauscle on the face is projecting. Two skin of maustache are coiling along the raised cheeks, Lips of mouth opening slightly, with smiling like experience. The whiskers is carved in fine curves. The face is depicted every finely well-proportioned and funny-looking. The white glaze is suffused with blue, and the face of glaze with fine veins. The roughcast is hard and perfect, first put on a larger of white make-up soil, then corved with clear glaze, last burnt. This is a masterpiece which unified the crafts of making porcelain with sculpture in the early period of the Tang Dynasty.

From the tomb, unearthed other vessels of white porcelain, a white porcelain Zun in shape of a child of the Western Regions, and a white porcelain bowl with design and high foot, which are graceful work of art.

白瓷胡人頭像
White Porcelain Figure of Hu's Head

三彩女立俑

唐（公元618年—907年）

通高44.5cm

1959年於陝西西安市中堡村唐墓出土

此俑頭梳鬢髮垂髻，微微舉目上仰，秀頰豐腴，粉面朱唇，柳眉宛轉，鳳眼含情，體態雍容華貴，舉止端莊大方，神情愜閑自若。身穿藍底黃花綢衣，內穿半臂，下着淺黃藍花長裙，裙腰齊胸，足蹬褚色尖履。兩手拱舉胸前，右肩斜披褚色披巾，顯得高貴矜持，幽雅恬靜，典麗柔美，風韵卓絕，洋溢着生命活力和青春之美。特別一對明眸，顧盼生輝，朱唇含笑，似喃喃細語，又似沉浸遐思之中，其神態給人無盡的美的享受。

三彩是唐代陶瓷工藝的一種新創舉。它以鐵、鋅、銅、鈷、錳等金屬氧化物配製釉料燒制而成，顏色鮮麗絢爛，融合自然。三彩女立俑鮮艷的衣飾與白皙的肌膚相映成趣，肥美的身軀和得體的舉止和諧統一，表現出內在的素養。整個造型比例勻稱，形神兼備，刻劃入微，在人物塑造上表現出"豐肌秀骨"的藝術風格，也反映出立俑作者觀察的細膩和技藝的高超。

三彩女立俑是一個盛唐美婦的典型形象，也是唐三彩女俑的藝術珍品。

Tri-colour Glazed Pottery Figure of Standing Woman

Tang Dynasty （618—907A·D·）

H·44.5cm.

Unearthed in 1959 in the tomb of Tang Dynasty at Zhongbucun, Xi'an City, Shaanxi

This figure with her hair combed into bun partly hanging down in coils, raising eyes slightly, looks beautiful with chubby checks and bright red lips, she appears calm, composed and dignified, the expression is carefree and leisurely. She wears blue coat with yellow flowers, with half of her arms exposed, and for the underwear. She has long skirt, light yellow in colour with blue flowers, the top of the skirt reaching the breast, with a pair of brown pointed-ends shoes. Her hands lifting in front of the chest, a longer reddish brown scarf draping on her right shoulder. She is noble, elegant, pretty and in a reserved manner, she is permeated with youthful vigour.

Tri-coloured is a new undertaking on the crafts of pottery in the Tang Dynasty. The glaze is mixed with the oxides of iron, Zinc, copper cobalt, manganese etc. then burnt, the colour is splendid and natural. The gorgeous garment of the figure with her white smooth skin, unified with the plentiful body and elegant manner, shows the beauty of her inner world. The shape is proportioned and lifelike, it's a graceful and splendid art piece.

This figure is a life mirror of a beautiful woman in flourishing Tang Dynasty, which is a precious gem of tri-coloured female figures.

三彩女立俑
Tri-colour Glazed Pottery Figure of Standing Woman

三彩女坐俑

唐（公元618年—907年）

通高48.5cm

1955年於陝西西安市郊王家墳唐墓出土

此俑頭髮上梳，旋成雙層扁高髻，黑髮粉面，身穿醬色袒胸窄袖襦衫，外罩白色錦褂，長裙高束胸際，裙裾寬舒，長垂曳地，領鑲醬色錦邊，衣綉八瓣菱形寶相花，袖邊爲綠色連續雙圈紋。綠色長裙作放射狀褶條，上綉柿蒂紋，腳穿雲頭鞋，端坐在藤編座墩上。座墩作束腰形，鑲嵌雙圈、寶相花和石榴花紋。左手作持鏡照面狀，右手伸出食指作塗脂狀。從儀態和服飾看，她是唐代宮廷的一名貴婦形象。

這件女坐俑，工匠們抓住了貴婦"對鏡貼花黃"的生活情景，以洗練明快的手法，重在攝取神態，表現出女俑的社會地位和高貴身分，刻畫了人物悠閑自得、矜持不凡的性格特徵。工匠對女俑的服裝着意給予裝飾、點綴和誇張，以綫條構成衣裙的外形，符合人體的曲綫美，給人大方優美的感覺，同時，配以瑩潤絢麗的彩釉和貼花裝飾，把寫意性和裝飾性、趣味性和時代性融爲一體，體現了較高的藝術追求。

Tri-colour Glazed Figure of Sitting Woman

Tang Dynasty（618—907）

H. 48.5cm.

Unearthed in 1955 at Wangjia fen, Xian city. Shaanxi.

The figure with her hair combed up and coiled in two-lager lofty black hair and pink face; ling skirt tied round her

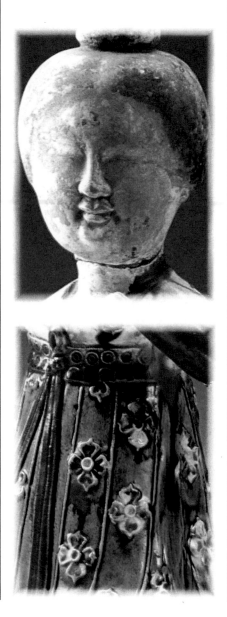

waist, with broad lower part spreading on the ground, she wears brown-sleeved shirt, which covered with white brocade coat; the collar inlaid brown brocade coat edge, on the frown embroidened octogonal flower disign, the edges of the sleeves adorned with green chained rings patterns. The green long skirt in radiate form shape, emnroideried the patterns of: the calyx of persimmon, wearing a pair of clound-top shoes, sitting on a stool which is wove with cane. The stool is thin in the waist, adorned with pomegranate patterns. Her left hand is in the shape of holding with a mirror, the right one streching it's index finger in the shape of applying powder and painting. According to her posture and gown, she was a nobleman of the royal place of the Tang Dynasty.

This figure the craftsman caught the nobleman's posture "making up in front of mirror", who made this figure with graceful method which shows the characteristic of care-free and elegant. The craftsman formed this figure in overstate and fine lines, adorned with splendid glazed flower, reflects the seeking on art of the craftsman.

三彩女坐俑
Tri−colour Glazed Figure of Sitting Woman

三彩三花馬

唐（公元618—907年）

高65cm，長80cm

1971年於陝西乾縣懿德太子墓出土

三花馬體形壯碩，骨肉勻停。馬頸微側，四足挺立，兩耳豎起，雙目有神。馬頸鬃毛剪留為"三花"，馬額鬃毛修剪成"劉海"。此馬通身施釉，背飾深綠色馬鞍，馬尾梳理打結上翹。頭部的籠套有綠色革帶，上飾黃色花朵，馬額、鼻梁和雙耳下方掛有杏葉形垂飾。馬身兩側革帶上也各飾有五枚杏葉形垂飾。

馬在唐代社會有突出的地位，在邊疆要塞，在征戰沙場，在宮廷禮儀，在商業貿易，在生產勞動，在游樂出行，都離不開它。因而，唐代養馬業十分發達。據載，唐高宗時，中央政府直接控制馬匹七十萬六千匹；唐玄宗時，御廄里畜有良馬四十余萬匹。唐詩中就有許多贊馬畫馬的內容。這件三花馬正是宮廷良馬的代表形象。鬃毛剪留"三花"，是宮中等級最高貴的馬的標志。

這匹馬塑造得十分健美。造型線條流暢，神完氣足，給人雄健奔放、飽滿瑰麗的印象。工匠抓住了馬的精神，馬頭微微偏側，這一扭動的神態，使線條挺拔、流利而富于變化，使形象生動而不呆滯，加之臀圓體壯，使內在的勁力活脫形外，表現出勃勃生氣，集中反映出唐代三彩馬釉陶藝術高超的技藝及成就。

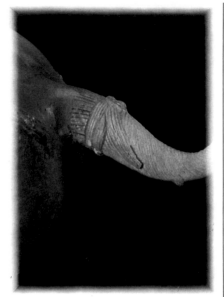

The Tri-colour Glazed Pottery Figure of a "Three Flowers Horse"

Tang Dynasty (618—907)

H. 85*cm L*. 80*cm*.

Unearthed in the tomb of crown price Yide at Qianxian County, Shaanxi in 1971.

This horse looks healthy and strong with proport oned muscle. The horse's neck turns slightly, four legs standing straightly, two ears pricked up and a pair of eyes staring piercingly. The horse's mane is cut into "three flowers" and the hair on the forehead, trimmed into bangs. The body is painted all over with glaze, on the back adorned with a blue-green saddle, a knot is coiled on it tail which is sticking upwards. There is green belt on the headstall, adorned with yellow flower design; adorned with decorations in apricot-leaf shape on the forehead and nose's bridge, under the two ears. There are five apricot-leaf decorations on each side belt of the body.

The horse had special important status in the society of the Tang Dynasty, it was used in many places, such as strategic pass, battlefield royal ceremony, commerial trading ect. In many poems of Tang Dynasty, there are many imscription about the horse. This horse is the typical image of the imperial best horse. the "threeflowers" on the mane is the symbol of the first class among the noble imperial horse.

This horse is formed gracefully and vigourously, the various lines shows a lifelike horse and expresses the energy of this strong horse, and it reflects the highest achievement ant skills in the tri-coloured glazed pottery figures making.

三彩三花馬
The Tri-colour Glazed Pottery
Figure of a "Three Flowers Horse"

三彩駝載奏樂舞俑

唐（公元618—907年）

通高56.2cm，長41cm；駝高48.5cm

1959年于陝西西安市中堡村唐墓出土

載樂駱駝造型精美，色彩艷麗，形象逼真，比例協調，生活氣息濃鬱。駱駝四腿直立，勁頸挺起，昂首上揚，張口嘶鳴。駝身施白釉，頸部上下、頭頂、尾巴及前腿上部長毛處施褚黃釉。雙駝峰上墊一平臺，上鋪向兩側下垂的長毛毯，周邊垂絲為茄紫色，毯身菱形格紋飾為錯落相間的褚黃及紫、白色。

駝背平臺上有七個男樂俑，背向盤腿環坐毛毯上，皆頭戴皂絲幞頭，腰系寬帶，身穿圓領窄袖長衫及翻領胡服。一人捧笙執簫，一人懷抱琵琶，一人欲吹排簫，一人手拿箜篌，一人持笛吹奏，一人欲打拍板。中間站立一女歌俑，鬢髮高髻，寬衣長裙，體態豐滿，作歌舞狀。載樂駱駝雄姿英發，似正伴着樂曲悠然前行，生動地再現了當年大漠絲路上的民俗風情。

據專家研究，從樂舞形象分析，應是盛行於唐開元、天寶年間的"胡部新聲"，它開始於新疆，后傳至甘肅河西，逐步溶入漢族舞樂特點，創造出新的舞樂，并進入宮廷。

這組駱駝載樂舞俑，是盛唐"絲綢之路"中西文化交流的見證，它使我們可以想象出作為國際都會長安當日的繁榮景象，也可印證出唐詩描述的"胡音胡騎與胡妝，五十年來竟紛泊"的歷史場景，還可理解到大唐開放的氣魄和中華文化的巨大包融能力。

Tri-colour Glazed Camel Carring Tri-colour Glazed Musician Figures

Tang Dynasty （618—907A.D.）

H. 56.2cm, L. 41cm, H. of camel 48.5cm.

Unearthed in 1959 at Zhongbucun, Xian City, Shaanxi.

This camel formed gracefully, is splendid in colour, life-like, proportioned, with thick life atmosphere. The four legs of the camel are standing strightly, with the neck holding up and the head is high, opening its mouth and weighing. The body is painted with glaze, around the neck, top of the head, the tail and the upper of the front legs are painted with brown, yellow glaze. On the hump of the camel, put a platform which covered with a long wollen carpet, the edge of handing thread are painted with purple glaze, the edge of handing thread are painted with yellow purple glaze and white glaze.

There are seven musician figures on the platform, they are circling in back to back and sitting on the carpet with coiling their legs , they wear the same type black scarfs on their heads, with wide ribbons around their waists, wearing long cobes with round collars and narrow-sleeved, and the gown of the Hu traditional. They play seven different kind of instrument and performing. In the central of the platform, standing a dancing female figure, with the hair tomed high into lofty bun, broaded-gown and long skirt, she is plentiful and in a posture of dancing. This group pottery figure is the witness of the exchanging of the culture between China and the Western Reigion in the flourishing Tang Dynasty, we might imagine that properious sight of the Chang An City at that time, and understand the great abilites in melting abroad culture of Chinese culture.

三彩駝載奏樂舞俑
Tri-colour Glazed Camel Carring
Tri-colour Glazed Musician Figures

三彩天王俑

唐 （公元618—907年）

高65cm

1959年於陝西西安市中堡村出土

天王俑形體高大，威風凜凜，是唐代新出現的一種殉葬俑。此俑身穿鎧甲，頭戴金盔，盔上有一大鵬金翅鳥。天王怒目圓睜，鼻翼上收，巨口開張，露齒若吼，左手叉腰，右手握拳，腳踏虯髯魔鬼，魔鬼鼓目咧呲，掙扎乏術。

天王俑的形象是按照傳說中的天神塑造的，是當世人們心目中嫉惡如仇、鎮妖驅邪的正義之神，是不可抗拒的力量和勇氣的象徵。工匠在塑造時，發揮了豐富的想象，運用誇張的手法，通過高矮強弱的鮮明對比，表達出正義必然戰勝邪惡的主題。此俑的造型刻意求工；面部威猛剛烈，肌肉突怒；體魄雄壯張揚，極具動勢，使人有呼之欲起的感覺。

天王俑屬唐三彩中的巨型雕塑類，以玄宗時唐墓出土最多。

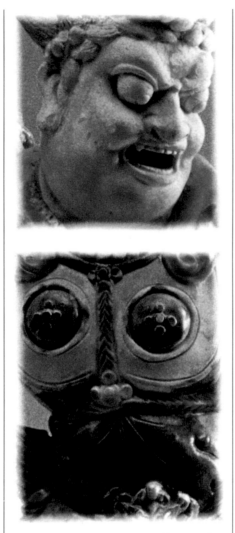

Tri-colour Glazed Pottery Figure of a Heaven Guard

Tang Dynasty （618—907）

H·65cm.

Unearthed in 1959 at Zhongbucun in Xian City, Shaanxi.

This figure of a Heaven guard has a strong body and is majestic-looking, which is buried figures of the Tang Dynasty. He wears armour with a gold helmet. The figure with his round eyes gogling angrily, opening the big mouth, showing the teeth as if shout, his left hand is sticking up the waist. the right hand clenching a fist, the feet are stepping a ghost with coiled whiskers, which is ferocious and no strength to struggle.

This figure is formed allow the Heaven god in the Chinese legend which is the god of the justice of Chiving out the ghost and protecing the people, which is the symbol of the bravery and power. The shape of this figure shows the topic of that the justice defeats the evil surely, with the overstate forming and clear constrast on size. This is a real guard to get rid of the ghosts.

This figure belongs to the sculpture in big size of the tri-coloured pottery of the Tang Dynasty, which were unearthed a great quatities from the tombs of the time of Xuanzong in the Tang Dynasty.

126

三彩天王俑
Tri-colour Glazed Pottery
Figure of a Heaven Guard

三彩鎮墓獸

唐 （公元618—907年）

高57.5cm

1959年于陝西西安市中堡村唐墓出土

鎮墓獸人面獸身。兩足前伸，軀體后蹲，昂首挺胸。肩生兩翼，翅羽開張；頭生兩耳，向外大展；額生獨角，直冲上方；額后束髮螺旋直上，背倚方戟。人面環眼怒視，鼻翼翹起，呲牙咧嘴，肌肉緊張，形象獰厲，神態威猛。

鎮墓獸是古代置于墓門內軀魔辟邪的葬品。用于保護墓室不受侵擾，佑庇亡靈平安升天。工匠采用浪漫主義手法，發揮豐富想象，造型上人獸結合，肩、耳及面部神情極盡夸張，造成令人膽戰心驚的威懾力量。鎮墓獸軀體穩健，靜中顯動，仿佛發現侵擾者，躍躍欲起，給人呲呲逼人的氣勢，有一種凜然不可侵犯的藝術感染力，也折射出大唐盛世意氣風發的時代精神。

Tri-colour Glazed Pottery Figure of a Tomb-guarding Animal

Tang Dynasty. （618—907）

H·57. 5cm.

Unearthed in 1959 at Zhongbucun, Xian, Shaanxi.

This tomb-guarding animal formed with a human face and monster body. Two feet are putting forward, and the body is squatting on the buttocks, holding up he head and chest. There are spreading wings on the two holding up he head and chest. There are spreading wings on the two shoulders; two ears extending outside; there is a lone horn on the forehead which is sticking to the sky; the hair is coiled upwards on the back of the head, with a halberd on its back. The round eyes are staring angrily, grinning and showing the sharp teeth, it is fercocious and majectic-looking.

The tomb-guarding animal was buried inside the tomb for getting rid of the evils in ancient time, and protecting the tomb without troubles, blessing the soul of the deceased person going into the heaven peacefully. The craftsman formed this figure with romatic and overstate method, unified the human face with the monster by his wonderful imagination, made a majectic-looking and fercoious tomb-guarding animal. This is a graceful figure which reflects the spiritual style of the flourishing Tang Dynasty.

三彩鎮墓獸
Tri-colour Glazed Pottery
Figure of a Tomb-guarding Animal

三彩塔式罐

唐　（公元618—907年）

通高69.5cm，口徑11.3cm，座底徑26.8cm

1959年于陝西西安市中堡村唐墓出土

三彩塔式罐由罐蓋、罐身、蓮瓣、底座四部分組成塔型器物。罐蓋蓋紐爲七層圓形塔頂，罐身多口，短頸鼓腹，罐肩塑有三個兩兩相間的龍頭和象頭，龍角高豎，象鼻長伸。罐與底座間飾三層仰覆蓮瓣，一層向上環抱，兩層向下伸展。底座是上小下大，呈喇叭形。四部分可分可合。

此罐造型奇特，結構復雜，制作精細，色澤艷麗。整個器形富于變化，具有節奏感和韻律美。黃、綠、褐、藍各色相間，釉色融合自然，斑駁陸離，顯得高雅富麗，光彩耀人。是三彩器中較爲罕見的作品。

塔式罐是一件生活用具，其工藝爲粘接成型。罐身用輪制，蓮瓣裝飾用捏塑，象首和龍頭則爲模制，然后用胎泥調成的漿泥一件件粘接成型。先經過素燒，再挂釉烘燒。工匠們技藝熟練，用彩很準，掌握了三彩釉的流動性能和胎體的密合性能，效果又美又雅，沒有釉層開片剝落現象，歷經千余年依然色鮮如新，器貌如初，反映出唐三彩精湛的制作工藝水平。

Tri-couloured Glazed Tower-shaped Jar

Tang Dynasty. （618—907）

H.69.5cm，D. of mouth 11.3cm. D. of base 26.8cm.

Unearthed in 1959 at Zhongbucun, Xian City, Shaanxi.

This jar is made of four parts, a lid , a jar, a waist in shape of lotus，a pedestal. The lid is in the shape of 7 layer ruound as the tip of tower；and the jar, with a flared mouth，short neck and three belly；on the shoulder of the jar，（with horns sticking up and trunks）three elephant heads and three feagon heads，alternating with each other，are arranging around the jar，with horns sticking up and trunks extending Between the jar and the pedestal，there are 3 layer lotus petal designs，one layer is up-ward，and two layers spreding downward. The pedestal is in the shape of a bell, the four parts could gathered or separted freely.

This is a unique style jar，the form is complexed，colour is splendid. The glaze is naturelly adorned with yellow，green，brown，and blue. This is a seldom seen and precious tri-coloured pottery figure.

This jar is a daily life vessel，which formed with pasting. The jar is made on wheel，decorations made by sculpture. The heads of elephant and dragon are made with model，then pasting them with the mud of rough cast on the jar. Firstly burning without glaze，then paimted glaze and burnt second time，this is a vigourous tri-coloured pottery jar in high level making skills，reflects the perfects crafts of tri-coloured of the Tang Dynasty.

三彩塔式罐
Tri-coloured Glazed Tower-shaped Jar

三彩獅子

唐（公元618—907年）

高19.8cm，底9.8cm

1955年於陝西西安市王家
墳出土

　　獅子全身踡曲，盤臥在不
規則平臺上。獅首轉向右側，兩
條前腿用力撐持，全身重心落
在兩只前爪及臀部三個支點
上。右后腿上抬，伸向嘴邊；左
后腿從前腿內側伸出，啃舐嬉
耍，一反日常給人威猛雄壯、凜
不可犯的姿態，顯得憨態可掬，
頑皮可親。

　　這件三彩獅子，是難得的
三彩動物精品。工匠在藝術上
熔鑄了南北精華，在北方原有
深厚勁健的基礎上，加進了南
方藝術中清新柔潤的特點。它
采用塑形、堆貼等方法，造型富
于變化，動態靈活自然。表現手
法以洗練明快為主，重在攝取
神態。我們從獅子安詳的舉止、
張開的蹄爪和以牙自我撓癢的
動作，不難看出工匠對生活的
觀察入微和高度的藝術表現
力。另外，獅子在燒制過程中，
釉色自然流動，互相浸潤，使整
個色彩流暢和諧，反襯出獅子
全身肌肉放松的效果，增加了
雕塑的情趣。

Tri-coloured Glazed Pottery Lion

Tang Dynasty. （618—907）

H.19.8cm. H. of pedestal 9.8cm.

Unearthed in 1955 at Wangjiafen, Xian, City, Shaanxi.

This lion, with its body rolled up and twisted and crouched on an irregular platform. Its head turns to the right, two forelegs supported itself up, the center of gravity is on the three surported points, its two foreclaws and its buttocks. the right hindleg lifted up highly, streching to its mouth; and the left one streched forward between its forelegs. The mouth is opening, biting its right foreleg gently, without majestic-looking of ordinary, shows honesty and loverly posture.

This figure is rare gem of tri-colour figures of animals. The craftsman unified the strength and thickness of the south, made this precious lion. It was made with sculpture. sticking etc. methods, formed vividly and naturally. According to the calm expressions and opened claws of the lion, and the action of itching with its teeth instead of its claw, we can find easily that the abilities of the craftsman is high and fine observing sight to the life. By the way, it was in the kiln of burning. The glaze was flowing natually, making the colour in harmonious way which reflects that all the muscles of the lion seem relaxed, adds the interest of the sculpture.

三彩獅子
Tri-coloured Glazed Pottery Lion

三彩假山水池

唐（公元 618—907 年）

通高 18cm，池寬 16cm

1959 年於西安市中堡村
唐墓出土

這件三彩假山水池是出土的一組三彩房屋模型里后花園中的陳設。假山峰巒層叠，高低錯落，樹木蒼鬱，山色凝碧。山間似有流動的雲彩，飛漱的清泉；山頂則有栖息的鳥兒，碩大的靈芝。山脚下，芳草萋萋，池水盈盈。兩只鳥兒是在池邊飲水，還是顧影自憐？整個作品秀雅的景致，充滿了勃勃生機，再現了大自然旖旎迷人的風韵。

三彩假山水池的層層山峰翠巒，是由雕塑手法塑成。工匠充分利用鉛釉的流動性，在無色透明釉上，滿山施以濃濃的翠綠色和醬褐色釉汁。在高溫焙燒中釉層熔融，任意浸漫，任意流淌，在雕塑的高低層面上，構成變幻自然的紋樣，使假山呈現出壯美的景色，體現出工匠們熟煉的技藝和較高的藝術素養。

墓中出土的房屋建築模型共八座，除假山水池外，還有小亭，說明了死者生前擁有豪華的宅第。

Tri-coloured Glazed Pottery Potted Landscape

Tang Dynasty（618—907）

H. 18cm, W. 16cm.

Unearthed in 1959 at Zhongbucun, Xian City, Shaanxi.

This potted landscape is displayed in the back garden of the tri-coloured glazed group of buildings models which unearthed from the tomb. The rockery has layers of ridges and peaks, higher or lower with dark green forest, the colour of the mountain is dark green. There is clear stream flowering in the mountain; on the top of the mountain, there are birds having rest, and big glossy ganoderma. At the foot of the rockery, grass is green, the water in the pool is clear. Two birds are drinking water by the pool. This landscape is graceful and elegant, full of life, reappears the beautiful sight of the nature.

The peaks and ridges are with the sculpture method. The creator made full use of flowing of the lead glaze, painted with high green and brown glaze on the clear glaze, in the burning of high temprature flowing, mixing freely, formed the magical natural veins on the face of the sculpture, let the rockery appear magnificent scenery, which reflects the high skill and abilities of art of the craftsman.

Besides the landscape, unearthed 8 building modles, there are small pavillion, which show the splendour of the residence owned by the master of this tomb when he was alive.

三彩假山水池
Tri-coloured Glazed Pottery Potted Landscape

青白釉雙龍柄瓷瓶

唐（公元 618—907 年）

通高 49.5cm，口徑 14cm，腹徑 25.5cm

1958 年民間征集

瓷瓶盤口，喇叭形長頸，頸上有兩道弦紋突棱。豐肩鼓腹，腹下內收，近底部微外撇。肩部有對稱的兩個雙龍柄，龍首獨角，雙唇緊緊銜住瓶口，龍身弓曲。龍首裝飾華美，制作精細。肩部飾高浮雕花瓣。

瓷瓶白胎白釉，胎質堅硬厚重，施釉不到底，釉層較薄，釉色白里泛青，釉質光潔溫潤。整個造形樸素優美，為隋朝和初唐時期流行的一種器形。它以旋、塑相結合。莊重古樸，剛勁強健，扣之有金石之聲。雙龍作柄在現存唐代器物中比較少見，1957 年西安市郊隋大業四年（608 年）李靜訓墓中曾出土一件白瓷雙龍雙腹瓶。根據造型特點，可能是專供祭祀或陳設用的陶瓷器物。

青白釉雙龍柄瓷瓶是唐代瓷器中一件珍品。

White Glazed Vase with Double-dragon Handle

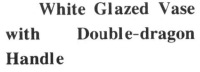

Tang Dynasty （618—907A. D.）

H. 49.5cm D. of mouth 14cm D. of belly 25.5cm

Colleted from the people in 1958

This vase has a falred mouth, with a long bell-shaped neck, on the neck, there are two protruding arrives. It has round shoulders and bulge belly, the lower belly is tightened inside, the base is in the shape of a bell. There are two symmetrical dragon handles on the shoulder, with single horn on ist head, two lips holding the mouth of the vase tightly, with the body benting. Decorations on the heads of dragons are graceful and splendid, which were made finely. On the shoul-

ders, adorned with flowers designs in relief.

This vase has white rought cast and white glaze, and the rough cast is hard and thick, the glaze didn't paint to the base, and the layer of glaze is thinner, the white glaze is suffused with green. The colour of glaze is bright and moist. The shape is simple and elegant, which is a popular vessel shape between the Sui Dynasty and the early period of the Tang Dynasty. It unified with sculture and whirling, the shape is simple and unsophisticated and vigourous, if you rap it, it would sound like a vell. The double-dragon handle is seldom seen on the vessels of the Tang Dynasty. There was a white-glazed double-dragon and double-bely vase, which unearthed in the tomb of Lijingxun who died in the 4th year of Daye of the Sui Dynasty (608A. D.) in 1957 at Xian City. According to the feature of the shape, this vase might be the pottery vessel for the feature of the shape, this vase might be the pottery vessel for the sacrifices or displaying.

This vase is a rare precious gem of the porcelains of the Tang Dynasty.

青白釉雙龍柄瓷瓶
White Glazed Vase with Double—dragon Handle

青釉倒装壺

北宋（公元 960 年—1127年）

高 19cm，腹径 14.3cm，底经 7.5cm

壺蓋與器身連為一體。蓋頂為柿蒂形，蓋把為一只鳳凰，鳳首伸出，鳳身彎曲成把柄，鳳尾飾連珠紋。壺嘴為一張口側臥的母獅，一只幼獅正在腹下吮吸乳汁。假蓋治飾一周連珠紋，假口治下飾一圈鋸齒紋。壺腹呈圓鼓型，布滿雕刻的纏枝牡丹團花紋。

青釉倒装壺呈橄欖色，造型獨特，構圖嚴謹，圖案精美。三朵盛開的牡丹團花用刀在坯體上刻出，刀法圓活流暢，裝飾效果強烈。鳳凰作把，獅子作流，想象豐富，神態生動，具有清新活潑的生活情趣。更具特色的是此壺的注水方式，注水口在壺底中央。注水時要將壺倒過來，注滿水后再翻過去，壺嘴正常出水而壺底不漏。原來，壺內有一個連接注水口的長注管，解決了不漏水的問題，這正是利用了"連通容器內液面等高"的物理原理，反映了工匠藝人巧思的科學性。

這件青釉瓷器產于"耀州窯"。該窯是我國北方著名的八大窯系之一，以生產工藝精湛的刻花青瓷馳名宋代。刻花技藝是先用刀具垂直刻出紋樣輪廓，再在紋樣旁用刀具斜刻，並剔去刀痕中的底泥，使紋樣微凸，然后施釉燒制。成品花紋清晰，層次分明，釉色晶瑩透亮，濃淡相間，有很強的立體效果。青釉倒装壺是耀州窯一件精采而罕見的珍品。

Green-glazed Dettle with a Bottom Inlet

Northern Song Dynasty (960—1127A. D.)

H. 19cm D. of belly 14.3cm D. of base 7.5cm

Unearthed in 1968 at Bin Xian County, Shaanxi

The body and the lid are in a whole shape. The top of the lid is the shape of a calyx of the persimmon, the handle is a phoenix in shape which streching its head, and the benting body is the handle, adorned with chains of rings pattern the tail. The mouth is a lying mother lion which is opening its mouth, and a young lion is sucking the milk under its mother's belly. Around the fake lid's edge, adorned with chains of rings patterns, under the fade edge, adorned sawtooth pattens. The belly of the kettle is bulge, adorned with peony flowers designs. This pot is olive green, the shape is unique, design is beautiful and vigourous. Three peonies were engraved on the belly , which are graceful and simple with perfect decorations. Taking the phoenix as the handle and the lion as the inlet, is lifelike and fantastic, with the fresh and vivid interest. The most important feature is the method of pouring water into, the inlet is in the central of the bottom. While pour water into, you should turn the kettle upside down. After it is full of water then turn it over again, and the water will be poured into the mouth normally and the bottom would be not leak. Originally, a long pipe which is connected with the inlet inside the kettle settles the problem of leaking, which is used the physical principle of "the surface of liquid is in the same hight inside the linking vessel." and which reflects the smart science of the craftsman.

The kettle was produced from the "Yaozhou Kiln". This kiln is one famours kiln of the eight kilns in the north of China, where was famous for producing graceful celadon in the Song Dynasty. Engraving is carved the pattern on the roughcast vertically at first, and then engraved by the pattern obliquely and rejected the mud in the lines, which made the pattern raised, at last pain the glaze and burnt. The finished products had perfect patterns, with crystal-like glace, alternating with thinner and thicker, with strong effects of three dimensional. This celadon kettle is one seldom seen precious gem of the celadons of the Yaozhou Kiln.

影青刻花梅瓶
Celadon Vase with Flower Pattern

相撲俑

金（公元1115—1234年）
高29.4cm；29.7cm
1986年於陝西渭南出土

二俑只穿褲頭，全身赤裸，兩腿叉開站立，扼腕護踝，雙手緊握，雙臂交于胸腹之間。環眼圓睜，雙唇緊閉，鼻翼似在翕動。一俑光頭，上身微傾，頭側向左；一俑蓄髮，正面站立，怒目而視。二俑造型寫實，體魄壯碩，活靈活現，似欲即將相撲，以決雌雄。

相撲是我國傳統的獨立競技項目。漢代稱為"角抵"，類似今天的摔跤。南北朝時（公元420—589年），分化成摔跤和相撲兩個獨立的競技活動。唐代發展成體育競技，始稱"相撲"。宋代每逢盛典宴會，宮中有"相撲"助興；南宋的臨安（今杭州市），已有職業相撲手。中國古典名著《水滸傳》中，就有專門描述燕青和任原相撲、李逵被相撲世家高手焦挺踢翻在地的精采記錄，說明相撲在民間已很流行。據《日本書記》載，相撲是奈良時代傳入日本，現在已經成為日本的國技。

日本相撲競賽是在高近一米、邊長六米的正方形賽臺上進行。參賽力士頭束髻角，腰系寬帶，跨襠兜一厚布，其它全裸。相撲時有"撞、推、拉、甩、絆"等四十八種撲法，一場平均十秒鐘左右，有的瞬間便可決出勝負。據專家研究，現代日本相撲與中國古代相撲有許多相似之處，中國古代相撲曾給日本相撲以很大影響。金代相撲俑的出土，反映了中國古代相撲的眞實形象。

Pottery Figures of Warestlers

Jin Period （ 1115— 1234A. D. ）

H 29.7cm；29.4cm

Unearthed in 1986 at Weinan City，Shaanxi

These two figures just wear underpants with the bodies bared, stepping apartly with the legs, with rings protecting the wrists and the ankles, their hands are cleaching tightly, their arms are crossing in front of the breasts. Their round eyes are goggling, closing their lips, the nostrils seem move. One of them is bareheaded, he is put forward slighty, and his head turn to the left; the other wears his hair, standing stea dy. glaring forward. These two figures form lifelike, with strong body are vivid looking as if start wrestle.

Wrestling is an traditional independent athletic event. In the Han Dynasty, whih was called " Jiao di " . like today's wrestling. In the southern and Norhtern Dynasties （420—589 A. D.）, which devided into wrestling and "Xiangpu" which are two independent athletic event. In the Tang Dynasty, which became the sports game and called " Xiangpu " （wrestling）.In the Song Dynasty, the palace would hold "wrestling"（Xiangpu）as enjoyment while ceremony；Lin An（Hangzhou City now）of the Southern Song Dynasty, had the wrestlers. There are brief inscription about wrestling in the famous classic work 《Tales about the hero》, which proved that wrestling was popular among the people at that time. According to the records of 《 The book of Japan》, the wrestling was disserminated into Japan at Nailiang Period, and now becomes the national athletic event.

Japan Style wrestling is carrying on a flatform which is one metre in height and the edge of the square is 6 metres. The wrestler coiled the hair into bun, tied a wide ribbon arornd the waist, and the cortch is wrapped with a coth, body bared. The wrestling has 48 kinds of action such as push, drag etc, one round about ten seconds, sometimes it could be decided the winner in a wrinkling. According to the research of experts, modern Japanese wrestling is quite similar with the ancient Chinese wrestling, the classic wrestling of China influenced greatly to the wrestling of Japan. The figures of wrestlers of Kin Period, mirrored the real form of ancient wrestling of China.

相撲俑
Pottery Figures of Warestlers

影青刻花梅瓶

南宋嘉泰四年（1204年）

通高33cm，頸高2cm，口徑3.5cm，肩徑17.5cm，底徑10.3cm

1972年於陝西略陽縣八渡河北岸出土

梅瓶小口短頸，寬圓肩，上腹豐滿，下腹內收，體勢修長，凹底。通體刻劃纏枝卷葉紋暗花。胎質堅致膩白，釉面明澈麗潔。

梅瓶是宋代瓷苑中出現的一種器皿。宋代社會，講究文化享受，都市提倡種草養花，蔚成風氣，梅瓶應運而生。

影青刻劃梅瓶造型端莊，色釉清雅。窯工技巧嫻熟，借助半深半淺的斜刀雕出立體裝飾紋樣，通過紋隙處積釉的深淺，表現若隱若現、光影迭錯的藝術效果，給人以靜中見動的豐富聯想和千姿百態的自然美感。

這件影青瓷釉層瑩潤，白中泛青，凹雕花紋四周及卷葉花紋，玲瓏活潑，略現青色，是"色白花青"產品，屬景德鎮名窯燒制。

影青刻花梅瓶的出土地略陽縣，地處秦隴蜀三省邊境，八渡河繞城東匯入嘉陵江。南宋時，抗金名將吳玠、吳璘扼守仙人關，略陽是后方戰略要地。與梅瓶先后出土宋瓷共33件，可能是當時富商官紳外逃時埋藏。

Celadon Vase with Flower Pattern

In the fourth year of Ji-atai (1204A. D.) of the southern Song dynasty

H . 33cm, H. of neck 2cm D. of moth 3.5cm D. of shoulder 17.5cm D. of base 10.3cm

Unearthed in 1972 by the river of Badu at Lueyang County, Shaanxi

This vase has small mouth and short neck, wide round shoulder, the upper belly is plentiful and the lower is extend inside, the shape is leader, with hollow base, engraved the branches and flowers designs on the vase. The roughcast is firm and fine white, the glaze is crystal-like and smooth.

This kind of vase is a vessel in the porcelain vessels of the Song Dynasty. In the Song dynasty, the people enjoyed the cultural taste, and the capital encouraged planting grass and flower, then this vase arised at the historic moment.

This celadon vase, the shape is dignified, the glaze is elegant. The creator is killed in making, which is expressed the effect of light and shadow, brightness or darkness with the help of the obliquely engraved designs and the deep lines heaping glaze, which shows the various and hundreds forms nartual beauty.

The glaze of the vase is crystal clear and smooth, white galze is suffused with green, the flower disigns engraved in hollow are vivid and graceful, shows green colour, which is the best peice of "white glaze and green flower", and belongs to the famous kiln of Jingdezhen.

It was unearthed at Lueyang county where is the border among the Shaaxi, Gansu and Sichua three provinces, the Badu river empties into the Jina Ling River around the east of the county. Two genarals Wu Jie and Wu Lin who fought against Jin and guarded the pass of Xianpen guan, which is the juncture of Lueyang County. Unearthed 33 peices porcelain vessels here, which might be hide by the rich and noble hurrily in escaping.

青釉倒裝壺
Green-glazed Dettle with a Bottom Inlet

描金孔雀牡丹紋執壺

明·嘉靖年間（公元1522—1566年）

高30cm，寬15cm，厚9cm，口徑5.9cm，足徑8.8cm

1959年底於陝西耀縣寺溝出土

壺由壺身和壺蓋兩部分組成。壺身為喇叭口，細長圓頸，扁腹圈足，頸腹之間安有對稱的扁把和細長流。蓋有子口，頂部隆起，蓋紐為一小獸蹲坐作回首張望狀。

壺的外壁通體以醬釉作地，扁腹兩側飾形狀相同的桃形開光，開光內飾孔雀和折枝牡丹。壺頸飾葉紋，流和把分別飾連弧紋與花卉帶紋，配之以窈窕秀美的壺體造型，顯得雍容華貴。圈足內心有青花"富貴佳器"四字銘文。整個紋飾纖細繁縟，圓活生動，布局嚴謹，疏密有致，對稱中有變化，以和諧求統一，給人富麗堂皇之感。

此壺用金粉作為彩料，在陶瓷器釉上描繪紋飾，稱為描金。據載，描金始于宋代。這一中國古代金彩裝飾，是將磨碎了的金粉倒入瓷鉢內，使之與水混合，直至水底出現一層金。使用時取其一部分，溶於適量的橡膠水，然后摻入適量鉛粉，再描繪到瓷器上，經低溫烤燒后，再用瑪瑙棒或石英砂磨擦，使其發光。這件執壺，是明代景德鎮彩瓷中的金彩瓷器。由於宋元燒造的描金器現存不多，而且金彩大多脫落，它現在仍光彩奪目，成為研究我國瓷器金彩裝飾工藝發展演變的重要實物，也是古代陶瓷珍品中一件十分珍貴的杰作。

Pot Traced Peacock and Peony Designs in Gold

Ming Dynasty, Jianjing Period (1522—1566A. D.)

H. 30cm, W. 15cm, Thickness 9cm, D. of mouth 5.9cm, D. of foot 8.8cm

Unearthed in 1959 at Sigou of Yao Xian County, Shaanxi

This pot is formed with two parts the lid and the body. The body has a flared bell-shape mouth, long slim neck, flat belly and ring foot. Between the neck and belly, laying symmetrical flat handle and a slim inlet. The lid has hole, and top is projecting, the knob is a squatting animal which turn back its head and watching in shape.

The outer of the pot is painted with dark reddish brown glaze, two sides of the belly, adorned with the same peach-shaped "kaiguang" area, inside it, adorned with the peacock and the branches of peony, adorned with leaf pattern on the neck; on the handle and inlet, adorned with chains of arc and fower designs, which are splendid and graceful with the unique slenden pot. Inside the central of the ring foot, there is a 4 characters inscription means that rich and precious vessel. The designs are fine and aerolaborate, with vigorous arragement, changing between the symmetry, shows the expressions of harmouny and splendour.

This vase's design is traced on the galze in gold, called "miao jin", which started from the Song Dynasty. This classic Chinese decorating method, is poured the smashed gold powder into a porcelain bowl, mixing with water, when used it, take some from the bowl, dissolved in certain rubber cement and added a bit lead powder, the traced on the vessel with it. Burnt with low temprature, polished with agate stick or quartz sand, let it be shinning. This piece, is a procelain traced in gold of Jingdezhen in the Ming Dynasty. Because lacking of the vessels traced with gold of the Song and Yuan Dynasty, and the gold fell mostly, but this is still shinning and bright, which is the important witness of the researching to the drafts of tracing in gold on China, and it is also a rare precious masterpiece of ancient chinaware.

描金孔雀牡丹紋執壺
Pot Traced Peacock and Peony Designs in Gold

五彩饕餮纹瓷方鼎

明代萬歷年間（公元
1573—1619年）

高12.8cm，口徑15.9×
12.8cm

1973年于陝西綏德縣溫家
原落雁砭出土

方鼎呈長方形，平沿方唇，
口沿兩側各豎一耳，下有四圓
柱形足。口沿下飾獸紋一周，腹
部貼橫印的獸紋及彩繪的饕餮
紋，由青花、黃、綠、紅、紫等
色彩繪成。四角及每面正中均
有一道扉棱，上飾"卝"紋。柱
足繪彩色環紋。腹底有方形青
花"茇"款。鼎腹內壁施白釉，略
呈淡青色，釉色細膩瑩潤。鼎上
紅彩釉呈赭色，紫色較少，青花
色澤淡而均勻，是明代景德鎮
窯少見的珍品。

此器由清代馬如龍夫婦墓
出土。墓主人馬如龍生前曾任
戶部江西司員外、江西巡撫等
職。康熙四十年（公元1701年）
時卒於任上，歸葬綏德故里。這
件五彩方鼎，可能是他在江西
任職時收集到的。

Multi-coloured Tripod with Animal and Ogre Pattern

Ming Dynasty, WanLi Period (1572—1619A. D.)

H. 12.8cm W. of mouth 12.8cm L of mouth15.9cm

Unearthed in 1973 at Wenjiaoyuan of Suide County, Shaanxi

This tripod is rectangle in shape, with flat edge and rectangle mouth, on the two sides of the mouth standing two ears, under the vessel are four pillar-shape feet. Around the vessel under the edge, adorned with animal pattern, on the belly adorned with animal pattern and taotie ogre pattern, which are unified with the clolour of green, yellow, red, purple, brown etc. There is one arrise in the middle of each side and on each corner, adorned with "卝" form designs. On the feet, painted with colourful ring patterns. On the base, with a character "茇" in blue as the symbol. Inside the belly, painted with white glaze, appearing light green, the glaze is fine and crystal clear. The red glaze on the vessel appears reddish brown, less of purple, green is light and well-distributed, which is rare gem of the chinawares of the Jongdezhen of the Ming Dynasty.

This vessel unearthed in the tomb of Marulong' of the Qing Dynasty. The master, Marulong, was the Minister of the JiangXi Province, who was died on his official in 40th year of Kangxi (1701 A. D.) then was buired to his home town Saide County. This tripod might be collected while he was on duty in Jiangxi Province.

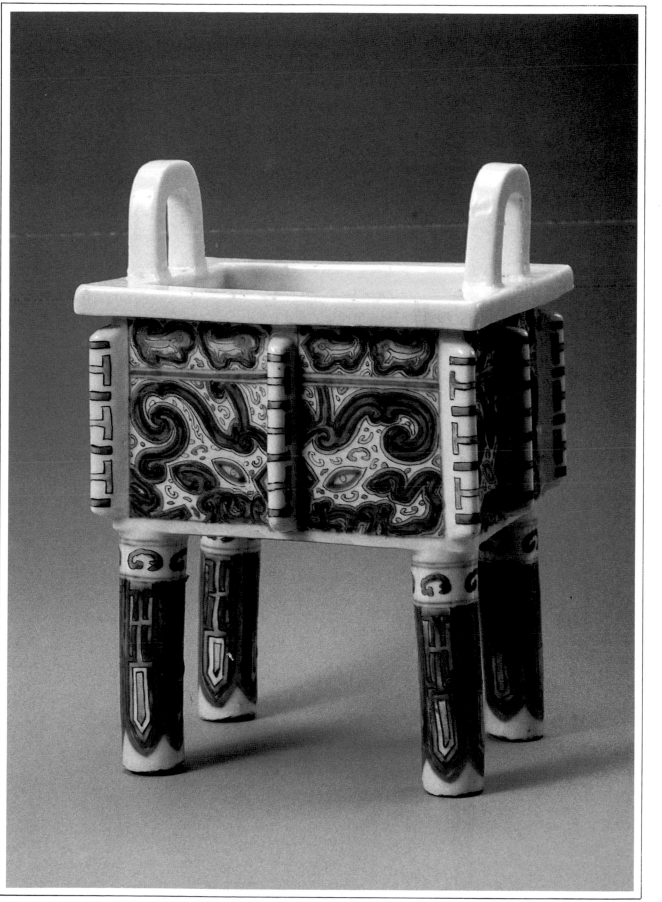

五彩饕餮紋瓷方鼎

Multi-coloured Tripod with Animal and Ogre Pattern

釉里紅僧帽壺

清（公元1636—1911年）

通高20.5cm，深17cm，口縱10.5cm，通流橫寬14.8cm，足徑8cm

此壺的口沿像和尚帽，由海棠曲綫圍成，前低后高。低處如長舌伸出作流。寶頂圓蓋上，也伸出長舌，與流上下相合。頭較寬，流下有一緩坡突出，與頭腹連為一體。腹部圓鼓較短，下腹急收，圈足略外侈。壺鋬扁薄稍寬，頂端有一如意頭，有孔，可用細繩與壺蓋相系。

僧帽壺通體遍飾折枝花卉，講究對稱。花枝細筆勾畫淡描，綫條生動流暢。花葉似菊，呈千層疊落花瓣。菊花象征經寒耐霜。此壺胎白質堅，釉面光澤瑩潤。其造型新穎別致，明顯受到外域器皿的影響。僧帽壺是元代創新的壺式，明清兩代仍有燒造，似為貯放奶液之類的盛器。

釉里紅是一種傳統的釉下彩繪瓷器。此壺先在瓷胎上用氧化銅描繪花紋，然后施以透明釉，入窯在1250℃左右的高溫還原火焰中一次燒成。由於燒造技術較難掌握，特別是銅元素對窯爐的溫度和氣氛要求非常嚴格，因此成功率比較低。我國人民以紅色代表吉祥富貴，釉里紅瓷器色調凝重華麗，正符合這種傳統審美心理，故深受人們的喜愛。

Underglazed Red Pot with Monk-cup Mouth

Qing Dynasty (1636—1911A. D.)

The mouth of this pot like cap of a monk, which formed with the curve of Chinese flowering crabaple, the front is lower and back is higher. The lower part like a long tongue is streching and connected with the inlet. The neck is wider, there is a slope projecting under the inlet, which connected with the belly. The bulge belly is short and the lower belly bent inside, the ring foot is flared. The handle is thinner and wider but flat, on which is a head with a hole, which could connect the lid by a fine string.

This pot is wholy adorned with flowers symmetrically. The lines of the flowers are thin and traced lightly, which are livedly and smooth. The leaf of the flower, like the chrysanthemum's formed as thousand layers petals. The chrysanthemum symbolizes undergoing the coldness and enduring the frost. The roughcast of this pot is white and hard, the glaze is smooth and crystal clear. The shape is fresh and unique, influenced by the vessel abroad obviously. This kind of vessel was created in the Yuan Dynasty, and still made in the Ming and Qing Dynasties, it seemed for storing the milk.

Underglaze red is a traditional underglaze painted vessel like this pot, at first painted the designs with the copper oxide on the roughcast, then painted on it with clear glaze, put into the kiln at 1250℃ reduction flame and burnt. It's very difficult for grasping the skill of making, especially the copper need the temparature and atmosphere strictly, so it's very difficult for getting a perfect ware. The Chinese peopel regard the red as the symbol of good fortune and richness, underglaze red chinaware, is in red splendid colour, it's fit for the taste of this traditional opinion, so it is deeply loved by the people.

釉里红僧帽壶
Underglazed Ret Pot with Monk-cup Mouth

脱胎粉彩碗

清·乾隆年間(公元1736—1795年)

高6.8cm,口径14cm,底径5.2cm

脱胎是創始於明代永樂年間的一種薄胎瓷。脱胎瓷薄如蛋殼,享有"薄如紙、聲如磬、明如鏡"的美譽。脱胎瓷的制作,從配方、拉坯、修坯、上釉到裝窯燒成,都有一整套技術要領和工藝要求。其中修坯一環最關緊要,一般要經過粗修、細修定型、粘接、修去接頭余泥、修整外形、蕩內釉,然后精修成坯并施外釉。在修坯過程中,坯體在利簍上取下裝上,需反復近百次之多,才能將2—3毫米厚的粗坯,修到蛋殼樣薄。其間,少一刀則嫌過厚,多一刀則坯破器廢,制作工藝難度極大。

此碗脱胎后,在器皿內外釉面上,用粉和彩料暈染作畫。碗內描繪春和景明時節田園生活畫卷:小橋流水,耕牛牧歸;春山叠翠,漁舟唱晚;花樹葱籠,開軒織布,一派安居樂業景象。碗外四周,山明水秀,或描繪石上對奕,籬畔吟讀;或描繪松下燒菜,高士扶杖;或描繪河曲垂釣,水上放舟;或描繪竹叢博古,文士賞畫。整個山水人物,畫筆纖細有力,畫面工整秀麗;薄胎釉白如玉,粉彩淡雅柔和,是一件十分精致細膩的藝術品。

脱胎粉彩碗底有"乾隆年制"青花雙框楷書款,系景德鎮官窯燒制的宮廷器物。碗上耕織圖紋飾,在瓷器上最早出現於康熙時期,康熙深知"農事傷則饑之本,女紅廢則寒之原",比較重視農業生產的發展。乾隆時期繼續實行獎勵農耕政策,并把耕織圖燒制在瓷版上,裱糊連結,制成折叠綫裝書。這件粉彩碗也反映出當時對農業的重視和社會安定的願望。

Eggshell Coloured Bowl with Scenery Design

Qing Dynasty, QianLong Period (1736—1795 A. D.)

H. 6.8cm D. of mouth 14cm D. of base 5.2cm

Eggshell porcelain was originated in Yongle period of the Ming Dynasty. Eggshell porcelain is as thin as the eggshell, which gained the honor of "as thin as paper, the sound like inverted bell, as bright as a mirror. " The making of the eggshell china, there is a whole complex group of key and points from the prescription, push, roughcast, reparing, painting glaze etc. The most important key is repairing the roughcast, formally through repairing roughly, repairing finely, sticking, get rid of the mud, restoring the form, swinging the interior glaze, and then repair perfectly as the roughcast and painted outer glaze. In the course of repairing, the roughcast get down and put on from the sharp basket, it would repeated at least one hundred times, the roughcast will be as thin as the eggshell from 2 — 3cm in thickness. In the process, less would be too thick, and much will be broke the roughcast, it is very difficult of making.

This bowl, after making the thin roughtcast, inside and outside the vessel, on the glaze painted with powder and colour. In side the bowl is a life scenery of spring: small bridge and the bright stream flowing, the ox is back after herding; the mountains are green in spring, and the boat is swinging under the sunset; the lady is wearing the cloth in the house which surrounded by the tall trees and flowers. Out of the bowl, bright hills and clear water, describing the playing chess, reading poems by the hedge; and describing cooking under the pine tree, the old walking with a stick, or telling about fishing by the river, or boating on the water; and telling about enjoying the antiques and paintings, the character and the scenery are vigourous and graceful; the glaze of the eggshell is as white as jade, the colour is gentle and elegant, it is a rare perfect precious work of art.

On the bottom, inscripted the 4 characters which told made in Qian Long Period, and which was produced by Jingezhen Royal Kiln made for the imperial use. According to the design of weaving shows the government took the developing of agriculture seriously, and the respecting of peaceful society life.

脱胎粉彩碗
Eggshell Coloured Bowl with Scenery Design

藍釉堆花瓶

清·乾隆年間(公元1736—1795年)

高40cm，口徑13cm，底徑12.3cm，腹頸19cm，腹深38.5cm

此瓶呈燈籠形。侈口，短頸，圓肩，圈足。瓶腹正面飾水仙、天竹、靈芝、翠鳥、蝴蝶，背面飾單株水仙。通體外施天藍釉，胎體厚薄適中，施釉較薄。瓶底下方中心有無方框篆款"大清乾隆年製"。圈足為泥鰍背，底足塗醬釉。

瓶腹所有紋飾全用堆貼手法製成。兩株水仙風姿綽約，一枝從下向上，舒展六條葉片，中間挺出三頭花朵，一頭怒放，兩頭待放；一枝從下向左，斜出六葉四頭。背面獨立一株水仙，四頭六葉，一頭綻開，一頭半開，兩頭含苞未放。一株天竹折枝向上，竹葉兩兩相對展開，三串果實累累，一隻翠鳥站立枝上，銜草振翅。一株靈芝茁壯茂盛，相伴而立。瓶頸一隻蝴蝶翩翩向下飛翔，肩部一隻蝴蝶款款飛向花叢。

藍釉堆花瓶釉色勻淨，淡雅悅目。在光線映照下，縮釉處微微泛黃。紋飾組合高雅和諧，寓意蘊藉。水仙雅稱"凌波仙子"，冰肌玉骨，儀態超俗，花開新春佳節之際，為吉祥之花。靈芝傳為長生瑞草，形似如意，為吉祥之物。天竹諧音"天祝"，蝴蝶翠鳥寓意美好吉祥，蘊含共祝吉祥如意。

堆花是清代出現的一種瓷器裝飾技法，它是在坯體上用筆蘸取同一泥料，堆出各種凸紋，造成浮雕效果，給人藝術感染。

Blue Glazed Vase of Flower Design

Qing Dynasty, Qian long period（1736—1795 A. D.）

H. 40cm D. of mouth 13cm D. of base 12.3cm H. neck 19cm Depth 38.5cm

This vase is in the shape of a lantern, with a flared mouth, short neck, round shoulders, ring foot. the frontal belly is adorned with narcissus, fish pelargonium, glossy ganoderma, king fisher and butterfly designs, the back belly decorated with single narcissus. The body is all painted with blue glaze, the roughcast is just OK, the glaze is thinner. Under the contral of foot, with a seal means produced in Qian Long period of the Qing Dynasty, the ring foot is the back of loach, painted with reddish brown glaze.

The designs of the whole body are made by heaping up and sticking up. Two narcissuse are slender, one of them is grown form the lower to the upper, with six spreading leaves, withing them are three flowers, one is in full bloom, the other two are booming; one branch grows six leaves and four flowers. The back side of the belly, one single narcissus, six leaves and four flowers, one of which is in full bloom, one is in half bloom, the left ones are not bloom yet. One fish pelargonium is grown upward, with symmetrical leaves spreading together, three bunches of fruits are great, one kingfisher standing on the branches, streching its wings and holding grass in its mouth. One glossy ganoderma grows sturdy by them. A butterfly flies downward on the neck, and a butterfly flies to the flowers on the shoudler.

This vase, the glaze is clear and smooth, which is elegant and good-looking. Jnder the sun light, the place gathering the glaze is suffused with light yellow. The designs are elegant and harmonious, with full meaning. The arcissus is called "Fairy maiden above the wave." Which is jade bone and ice skin, appears in all her glory, is a lucky-plant. The fish pelargonium has harmony in Chinese character means "heavenly blessing", butterfly and kingfisher means happiness and good fortune, which is meaning of blessing good luck and happiness.

Heap up flowers is a new decoration on the chinawares in the Qing Dynasty by which makes the projecting designs like releif, let the design graceful and splendid.

藍釉堆花瓶
Blue Glazed Vase of Flower Design

永泰公主墓宮女圖

唐神龍二年（公元706年）
高176cm，寬196.5cm
1960年於陝西乾縣永泰公
主墓發掘出土

　　永泰公主（公元684—701年），名李仙蕙，字秾輝。唐中宗李顯第七女，唐高宗李治和武則天的孫女。大足元年（公元701年），年僅17歲的公主因私議祖母，觸犯武后，與其夫武延基同被逼令自殺。中宗復位後，公元706年陪葬乾陵。

　　宮女圖原繪於前墓室東壁之東側。九位宮女高髻便妝，豐肌秀骨，在為首宮女的引領下，緩步徐行，侍奉公主安寢。宮女高髻多種多樣，有盤旋上卷的螺髻，有兩歧分縱的雙髻，還有半翻髻、回鶻髻驚鵠髻等，為首者髻高逾常。髻上不施金翠花樹，不戴寶鈿簪珥，樸素無華，大方明净。宮女上著窄袖短襦，酥胸微露，肩披長巾，羅裙曳地，足着高翹雲頭履。她們各司其事，或捧玉盤，或持紈扇，或攜拂塵，或端妝盒，或舉燭臺，或拿如意，或抱食盒，或執玻璃杯。為首一人則手挽紗巾，置於腹前。她們年齡不同，表情各异，有的神態安詳，有的秀眉緊鎖，有的若有所思，有的明眸憂戚，有的默然自若，有的顧盼低語，其儀容嫻静肅穆，體態輕盈活潑。

　　宮女圖表現人物群體關係，技藝卓越。行進行列參差錯落，層次有序，描繪人物無論正面側面，還是背面，相互呼應，生動入微，在畫面安静無嘩的行進中，似聞羅裙輕微的悉索之聲。從宮女的容貌和體態，反襯出她們所處環境的莊重森嚴，而那猶帶稚氣、秀潤可愛的面龐，又掩蓋不住她們青春的活力和生命的躍動。特別是手執高足杯的少女，蛾眉秀目，婀娜多姿，“S”型體態，卓然超群。她頭梳高螺髻，身穿淡綠短襦，披肩繞過雙肩，自然披於胸前，綠色長裙曳地，纓帶悠悠下垂，其神朵照人，呼之欲出，宛如一個美的化身。畫幅上的宮女，人物造型十分準確，人體比例恰到好處。衣裙綫條，勾勒精當，揮灑自如，筆力遒勁，氣韵貫通。這種富於彈性和質感的鐵綫描，有的竟長達一米二以上，依然流利圓勁。畫師深厚的功力和藝術造詣，讓人驚訝嘆服。

　　這幅唐墓壁畫，因時隔一千多年，顏色多已剝失變色。它既不像敦煌石窟壁畫那樣富麗，也不像唐代卷幅那樣纖細，但它却以清新健美的格調，給人強烈的藝術享受。宮女們被描繪得細膩精致，形神兼備，實為唐墓壁畫的藝術精品和上乘之作，它為研究唐代歷史和宮庭生活，提供了極為珍貴的形象化實物資料，也為東方乃至世界藝術畫廊增添了輝煌瑰麗的光彩。

Maids of Honour

In the second year of Shen Long of the Tang Dynasdty (706 A. D.)
H. 176cm W. 196.5cm
Untearthed in 1960 from the tomb of Princess Yong tai, Qian Xian county, Shaanxi.

Princess Yongtai, （684—701 A. D.）names Lixianhui, she was the 7th daughter of the Emporor Zhongzong Lixian, the grand daughter of Empress Wuzetian. First year of Dazu (701 A. D.) 17—yesr-old princess were ordered committed themselves suicide with her husband Wuyanji, because of talking about her grand mother Empress Wuzetian. After Zhongzong returned his throne, let her buried at QianLing Mausoleum in 706 A. D.

This mural originally painted on the east side of the east wall of the frontal tomb. Nine maids of honour with high hair bus and dress in normal, with plentiful skin and full face also pretty. They are serving the Princess sleeping following a pretty maid. The hair form of their are several kinds, there are coiled bun in snail, double bun apartly, etc. The first maid's hair bun is the most high and lofty. There is no decorations on the hair, simple and elegant. They wear gown with short sleeves, show their smooth skinned chests, covering the long scarves on their shoulders, the long silk skirts spreading on the ground, wearing pairs of raised-top shoes. They served in the own thing, holding jade plate, handing the fan, taking the horsetail whisk, holding the make-up case lifting the candle, or getting the food case or handing the glasscup. The first one drew the silk scarf, put in front of the chest. They've in different age, expression, some are peaceful, some are knitted brows, some are thinking over, some are carefree, they are in silent manner and postures are light and vivid.

This mural expressed the group of maids, in superb crafts. The tracing no matter how about the face, the side, the back, which are in whole form, vivid like and portraying finely. In the silent process of the mural, it seems there being the sound of the silk gowns. From their face feelings and posture, reflect the atmosphere being dignified and stern, and those faces with childishness are pretty and smooth-skinned, which would not cover their youthful life and activities of life. Especially, the girl who holding the high foot cup, bright eyes with pretty brows, pretty and refined, "S" form posture is superb graceful; the scarf circling the shoulders and hanging down in front the chest naturally, the green long skirt spreading on the gourn, the silk ribbons dangling freely, as if she would go out from the mural like a real pretty girl. The shape of the maids on the mural are perfect and proportioned. The lines of the garments and skirts, tranced finely and gracefully which are vigourous and smooth. This kind of iron line tracing is full of spring and gracefulness, some of them over 1.2 metres long, still fluent and round. The ultility and the attainments of the pointer are surprised by the greatness and fantasia.

After thousand years, this mural's colour mostly peel off. It is not as splendid as the Dunhuang's frescoes, neither as the fine as the paintings of the Tang Dynasty, but it still kept the fresh and graceful style, shows expressions of the enjoy of art. Those maids of honour are described finely and gradcefully, form and spirital detail are here, which is rare masterpiece of the frescoes of the tombs of the Tang Dynasty' which supplies the materials of researching the imperial life and history of the Tang Dynasty, also adds the splendid colour for the east and the world gallery.

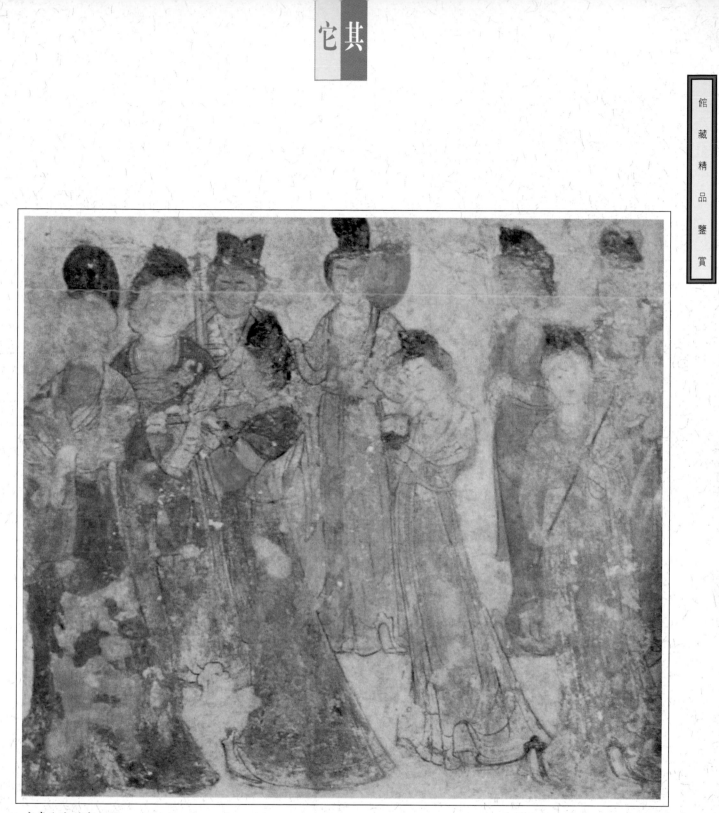

永泰公主墓宫女图
Maids of Honour

章懷太子墓禮賓圖

唐睿宗景雲二年(公元711年)

高184.5cm，長252.5cm

1971年於陝西乾縣章懷太子墓出土

章懷太子(653—684年)名李賢，字明允，是唐高宗李治與武則天的二兒子。上元二年(675年)立為太子，調露二年(680年)被廢為庶人，開耀元年(681年)流放巴州(今四川巴中縣)，后被逼自殺。中宗復位后，于神龍二年(706年)以雍王身份陪葬乾陵。景雲二年(711年)，以章懷太子身份與房氏合葬。

禮賓圖位于章懷太子墓道東壁。畫面上共有六人，前三人頭戴介幘籠冠，身穿紅色長袍，腰束寬帶，綬帶曳地。一人手執笏板，正與另外二人交談商議。他們舉止穩重，雍容大方，應是唐朝鴻臚寺的官員。緊隨其后三人是外來客使，頭一位身穿翻領紫袍的脫髮者，深目高鼻，濃眉闊嘴，微微欠身前趨，雙手叠置胸前，從面相和服飾推測，當是東羅馬帝國的使節。第二位身穿寬袖長袍頭戴羽毛冠者，束白帶，穿黃靴，靜靜侍立等待，雙手拱於袖中，當是高句麗國(今韓國)使節。后一位身穿圓領灰氅頭戴雙耳皮帽者，稍稍靠后恭立，雙手拱于袖內，當是吐蕃使節。三位禮賓靜候安排，神情肅然。

這幅禮賓圖是唐朝對外開放，頻繁外交活動的形象記錄。長安作為大唐首都，成為中外交往的歷史舞臺，各國使節紛至沓來。據史載：從永徽二年(651年)到唐末，大食國(即阿拉伯帝國)通使中國達三十六次之多。武則天時，阿拉伯人僑寓廣州、揚州和泉州諸港者，數以萬計。東羅馬帝國曾七次通使中國。西安何家村發掘的唐代皇室窖藏中曾出土一枚東羅馬拜占庭希拉克略金幣，也為唐朝與東羅馬交往提供了實物證據。

這幅禮賓圖，具有強烈的寫實性和濃鬱的生活氣息，人物造型準確，綫描技藝精湛，客使的面部和服飾勾劃得細膩逼真。衣紋用綫剛柔相濟，一氣呵成，具有大家風範，特別人物眼睛描繪得十分傳神，把特定環境下的人物身份、氣質、性格、心情表現得恰如其分，有很強的感染力，是唐墓壁畫中的傑作之一。

Trating Foreign Friends

In the second year of Jingyun of Evporor Ruizong (711 A. D.)

H. 184.5cm L. 252.5cm

Unearthed in 1971 at the Tomb of Prince Zhanghuai of Qian Xian County, Shaanxi.

Prince Zhanghuai, named Lixian (653—684 A. D.), who was the second son of Emporor Gaozeng, and Wezetian. In the second year of Shangyuan (675 A. D.) he was ordered to be Crown Prince, and in the seocnd year of DiaoLu (680 A. D.) he was banished to the Bazhou (Bazhong county, Sichuan), and later he was forced to commit himself suicide. After Emporor Zhong zong came back the thone, he was buried in the QianLing Maosolenm with the status of King Yong in the second year of ShenLong (706 A. D.). In the seocnd year of JingYun (711 A. D.), he was buried with his wife Fang's together with the status of Crown Prince Zhanghuai.

The fresco located on the east wall of the tomb's passage. There are six persons on the painting, the frontal three ones wear lofty hat, and red long cobes, tying wide ribbons around their waists which are dangling the ground. One of them handing a tablet before his breast, who is discussing with the other two. Three persons following them are the guests from the other countries, the first one is bald and wears purple robe with turning collar, with deep eyes and high nose, big mouth and heavy eyebrows, extending his body forward, two hands putting before the breast, judging from his appearance, he is the envoy of the Easter Roman Empire; the seocnd one wearing the feather hat, tying white ribbon, with yellow robe, waiting silently, two hands crossing in the sleeves, who is the envoy of the Korea. The last one wears gray robe with round collar and a double-ear leather hat, a little bit backward standing still, two hands streching in the sleeves, who is the Tibet. Three foreign guests are waiting for the arranging silently, with serious feelings.

The fresco is the life recording of the opeing abroad, frequent foreign affiars of the Tang Dynasty. Being the capital of the Tang Dynasty, chan'an became the stage of the foreign affairs, the envoies of all the countries gathered here. According to the historical recordings: from the 2nd year of Yonghsui (651 A. D.) to the end of the Tang Dynasty, the Arabian empire sent envoy to China about 36 times. At the time of Wuzetian, ten thousands of Arabian lived in Guangzhou, Yongzhou and Quanzhou cities. The Eastern Roman Empire once sent 7 times envoy to China. A gold corn of the Byzantine Empire of the Eastern Roman which unearth in Xian city, supplied the witness of the contact between the Empire Tang and the Eastern Roman Empire.

This fresco, with thick life taste and strong realistics, the person are portrayed correctly, propositioned, the garments and the faces are described vividly and finely, the crafts of tracing the lines is superb, which used fluent lines and painted within one breathe, it's the masterpiece. The eyes of the envoies, described perfectly, which reflected the uniques status and characteristics, feelings etc, with the simple and graceful lines, it is rare superb work of the frescoes of the Tang dynasty.

章懷太子墓禮賓圖
Trating Foreign Friends

狩獵出行圖

唐睿宗景雲二年（公元711年）

高 100—200cm，全 長 890cm

1971年於陝西乾縣章懷太子墓出土

畫面共有四十多個騎馬人物。前面四匹輕騎開道，后面兩匹駱駝載運輜重。隊列中一人持旗，數十騎左右并列，參差錯落，簇擁一位身著長袍、騎一高頭大馬的主人，正在向前馳驅。周圍山岳起伏，林木掩映，構成一幅場面宏大的狩獵出行圖。

這幅壁畫畫面構圖完整，造型生動準確，布局疏密相間，幾十個人物和鞍馬不是靜態的羅列，而是在奔馳追逐中造成強烈的動勢。鞍馬人物各具形態，有的伏背勒繮，有的怒目策馬，有的臂上架鷹，有的懷中抱犬，有的回首呼喚，有的側身顧盼。駿馬勁健，四蹄騰空，旌旗獵獵，煙塵滾滾。整個畫面人馬互為呼應，氣氛熱烈緊張。畫師把狩獵出行的霎那情景，濃縮筆端，給以典型化的表現，留給后世永久的動勢美。色彩運用暈染方法，處理明暗關係，生動地表現了物體的質感。

唐代詩人張祐有一首《觀獵詩》："晚出郡城東，分圍淺草中，紅旗開日來，白馬驟迎風。"詩中描繪的情景與此圖描繪的情景頗為相似。狩獵是唐代繪畫表現的重要題材，許多名家繪畫俱已失傳。狩獵出行圖不僅使我們形象地感受到了唐代狩獵的真實情況，更以它高超的藝術成就為中國美術史增添了不朽的篇章。

Going Out for Hunting

The 2nd year of JingYan of Emperor Ruizong.（771 A. D.）

H. 100 — 200cm L. 890cm

Unearthed in 1971 from the tomb of Crown Prince Zhanghuai at Qian Xian County, Shaanxi.

There are over-forty figues riding on the horses. Four light riders are clearing the way in the front, at the back two camels are carrying the baggages. One of the group holding the flag, about ten rides walking balancedly in the right and left, who coustering round a master who rides a strong horse and wears long robe, running forward. The hills and forests surrounding them formed a grand going out for hunting.

The form of the fresco is graceful and perfect, and the forty riders are not in the silent posture but in running or chasing posture. The horses and persons are in different form and postures, several holding the halter, several are riding fastly. Some holding the egle on their arms, some clustering the dogs, some shouting and turning back, some turning to the side and watding. The horses are strong, and the flags are waving in the wind, dusty is billowing. The atmosphere of it is vigourous and the horses are echoing with the riders. The painter collected the typical scenery of the hurting in his brushes, then described in brief and graceful lines, left us a great work. He expressed the vivid scenery of the hunting using the colouring and dealing with the brightness and darkness.

'Several poems of the Tang Dynasty describing the scene vividly which are similar with this fresco. The hunting is the important material of the paining of the Tang Dynasty, most works of the famous painters had not be handed down. This fresco is not only show the real scene of the hunting of the Tang Dynasty, and also is the great masterpiece of the Chinese fine art history.

狩獵出行圖
Going Out for Hunting

馬球圖（局部）

唐神龍二年（公元706年）

高196cm　寬154cm

1971年於陝西乾縣章懷太子墓出土

　　馬球圖是唐章懷太子李賢墓道西壁的組畫之一。原圖場面宏大，有二十幾匹駿馬追逐奔馳，馬尾結紮；騎馬者頭戴幞巾，身穿窄袖袍服，足蹬長靴，手持球杖。有激烈爭球的場景，有騎馬觀戰的場景，也有奔馳前來參戰的場景。這個畫面表現的是正在賽球的情景：最前者手持球杖，作反身擊球狀，其餘4人策馬奔突，持杖作迎擊狀。畫工把爭球瞬間的氣氛，通過動態的生動刻劃，表現得十分逼眞。

　　馬球原名波羅球，是從波斯傳入我國的一項運動。馬球又稱擊鞠，是一種馬上球戲。騎馬者以鞠杖擊球，以先入網為勝，名「頭籌」，得籌可以唱好。唐太宗時命專人習波羅球，當時長安升仙樓外就有外國人擊球。由於唐代帝王的酷愛和提倡，馬球運動曾盛極一時，上至天子，下至軍士，都十分喜愛。唐玄宗就是一名馬球高手，他在景雲中作臨淄王時，曾受命與迎接金城公主的吐蕃馬球隊較量。他僅帶領三人，與吐蕃十人「東西驅突，風回電激，所向無前」，取得勝利，為唐朝爭得榮譽，傳為歷史佳話。宣宗、僖宗都是名手，穆宗、敬宗也酷嗜球藝。玄宗時諸王駙馬都爭築球場，文宗時三殿十六王宅都可打球，平康坊還有專門的球場。左右神策軍里都有擊球高手，文人學士也以能打馬球為能事。這幅馬球圖則形象眞實地記錄了一千多年前的唐代馬球運動的情景，為我們了解馬球這一體育競技提供了寶貴的資料，也是一幅難得的藝術珍品。

Playing Polo（part of it）

In the 2nd year of Sheng-Long of Tang Dynasty（706 A. D.）

H. 196cm　W. 154cm.

Unearthed in 1971 at the tomb of Crown Prince Zhang huai, Qianxian County, Shaanxi

This fresco is one of the frescoes on the West Walls of the tomb passage inside the tomb. The original fresco is grand, over twenty horses chasing and running, the tails of them are wiled; the riders are wearing the scarfs covering their hair, with robes and long shoes, handing the sticks. There are different scences, the intence snatching polo, watching on the horses, and running for helping the game. This part is about the scene of playing polo; the frontal one handing a stick in the posture of beating the polo, the other four persons are running with their horses, holding the sticks in the posture of meeting head-on. The painter described the second with vivid lines and expressed true to life.

The game originally named polo, which is a game propagated from Bersia, Which also call "ju", a kind of game on the horse back. The rider beats the ball by "ju" stick, earlier inside the net is winner, called "first-rate", and got prize. The emperor Tai Zong of the Tang Dynasty ordered the person trained to play polo, and at that time some foreigners playing polo out the "pavillion of Shengxian" at Changan. Because the emperor loved and encouraged this game, the polo was popular, from the emperor to the soldiers, both liked the game. The emperor Xian Zong was a high-class player of polo, who was the King of Linzi in the Jingyun period, who was ordered to fight against the polo team of the Tibet who were meeting the Princess JinCheng. He only lead three men, against with ten men of the Tibet, and they running east or west, at last, gained the game and win the honour for the Tang Dynasty. The emperor Xuan Zong, Xizong were famous players, Muzong and Jingzong liked the polo very much. At the time of Xuan Zong Period, many kings built the field of playing polo, Wenzong period, the residence of the Kings could playing polo inside, and there was specialized field for playing game at Pingyuan Fang. Among the royal army, there are good players, the scholars also play polo well. This frecso recorded the real scene of the playing polo of the Tang Dynasty thousand years ago, supplies precious objects of knowing the polo game, and it is rare precious.

馬球圖
Playing Polo

觀鳥捕蟬圖

唐睿宗景雲二年（公元711年）

高168cm　寬175cm

1971年於陝西乾縣章懷太子墓出土

觀鳥捕蟬圖繪於章懷太子墓前室西壁南側，畫面表現的是唐代宮女戶外悠閒散步的倩影。為首一人頭梳高髻，面龐豐腴，身穿黃色衣裙，肩披絳灰披巾，雙手挽巾胸前，站立樹前，目視前方，若有所思；中間的宮女，頭梳雙螺髻，身着男裝，足蹬便履，正躡手躡腳、小心翼翼地去撲捉秋蟬；后一位宮女頭梳高髻，肩披朱紅長巾，左手托巾，右手執釵，正仰觀低飛的鳥兒。三位宮女形象，神態不同，身姿自然，與驚鳥鳴蟬，互相呼應，組成一幅宮庭生活的風俗畫。作者刻畫人物細膩逼真，表達了長期幽處深宮的婦女的寂寞心境和對自由的渴望心情。

Watching the Bird and Catching the Cicada

In the 2nd year of Jing yun of the Tang Dynasty（711 A. D.）

H. 168cm W. 175cm.

Unearthed in 1971 at the Tomb of Crown prince Zhang huai，Qianxian County. Shaanxi

The fresco was painted on the south side of the east wall of the fontal tomb's chamber，which shows the scene about the maids of honour who wandering carefree. The frontal maid with the hair combed into a lofty bun，her face is plentiful，wearing yellow garment，drapping a gray cape，hands are crossing before chest，standing in front of the tree，watching forward；the middle one，with the double-snail bun of her hair，dressing in man's style，with normal shoes，who is catching the cicada carefully and walking gingerly；the last maid with lofty bun，drapping a red long scarf，left hand holding the scarf，and right hand holding a hairpin，looking up to the flying bird. These three maids are in different posture；naturally，combinated a whole genre painting with the flying bird and cicada. The painter described the maids finely and vividly，espressed the feelings of the miads who imprisoned in the Palace for ages and long for the nature.

觀鳥捕蟬圖
Watching the Bird and Catching the Cicada

骨雕人頭像

新石器時代（約1萬年—4千年前）

高2.5cm

1982年4月14日於陝西西鄉縣何家灣出土

人頭像是先民們用獸類肢骨雕成。上寬下窄，呈倒梯型。頭的上部利用骨節磨平，似小帽扣頂，因年久朽爛，頭頂出現空洞。額頭凹進，眉骨微起，眼眶下陷，眼珠如圓球凸出，鼻似蒜頭，高高隆起，嘴唇寬厚，嘴巴凸起，整個表情似瞑目沉思狀。

這個骨雕人頭像距今約6000多年，是目前我國發現年代最早的骨雕作品，它為研究我國骨雕藝術提供了珍貴實物。骨雕人頭像比較完整，五官位置比較準確，制作手法古樸、粗獷，神態憨厚莊重。從脖頸有斷裂痕迹推斷，可能原來還有身體部分，構成人體立雕。

雕塑是一種空間藝術形式，給人以立體的美感。一件雕塑作品往往積澱着歷史的烟雲，反映出當時的社會生活，濃縮着一個時代的人們對美的追求和向往。新石器時代的先民們以極其落後的生產力，在同嚴酷的大自然進行搏斗，從而謀求生存時，就地取材，創造了這件作品，盡管稚拙古樸，卻表達了一種對祖先的崇拜。可能把它供奉在專門的地方，受族人膜拜，以祈求神靈保佑部族的人丁興旺。

從骨雕人頭像出土的地層看，屬何家灣新石器時代遺址仰韶文化半坡類型的早期遺迹。

Hear of Bone Carving

The Neolithic Age（About ten thousand years—4000 years ago）

H. 2.5cm.

Unearthed in 1982，April at Hejiawan of Xixiang County，Shaanxi.

This head figure was carved with animal bone by the ancestor. The shape is wider upper and narrower lower, formed in a upside of a ladder-shaped shape. The upper part of the head is polished by the joint; like a cap covered the head, because long vears of rottening, empties in the top of head. The forehead is hollow, the euebrow bone is projecting, the orbit is trapped down, the eye-ball like the projecting balls, the nose like a garlic which raising high, the lips are thick, month is projecting, the expression like closing eyes and thinking.

This bone head was made 6000 years ago, which is the earliest piece of bone carving unearthed in China, which is the witness of the researching Chinese bone carving, It is finished, the facial features are propotioned, the making method is brief and rough, the expression is honest and dignified. Judging from the rift on the neck, which might be connected with the body.

Scuppture is a kind of art of space, shows the beauty of three-dimensional. Generally, one sculpture gathered the vapour of the history, reflected the society life of that time, concentrating the seeking beauty of one time. The ancestors of the Neolithic Age used the lag behind. Productive forces, fighting against the crue nature, and while make a living, they got the material and created this jade carving. Although it is simple and clumsy, it shows the worthip to the ancestor. It might be displayed at special places for paying homeage and blessing the people in good luk and population flourishing.

Accolding to the earth of which head unearthed, it is the earlier size of Yangshao Cultural of Banpo in the Neolithic Age.

骨雕人頭像
Head of Bone Carving

玉雕人頭像

新石器時代（約1萬年—4千年前）

高4.5cm

1976年於陝西神木縣石苑龍山文化遺址出土

玉人頭為側面頭像，由雙面平雕而成。頭頂有高高束起的髮髻，團型臉，鷹勾鼻，大鼻翼，嘴巴半張，下唇較長，腮部鼓起，根據材質使耳朵偏后，一只綫刻大眼刻於額頭稍后部位，幾乎占據一半地方。面頰有一透鑽的圓孔，下方是短細的脖頸。

此頭像側面似一壯年男子，剛健而憨厚。額、鼻、嘴、耳輪廓綫弧度具體明確，眼睛用單條陰綫刻成，位置明顯夸張，給人具像和抽象結合的美感。早在距今4900—4100年的先民們對藝術的感受和表現，留給我們無盡的遐想。這件裝飾品也使我們看到了人類文明曙光的出現。

此玉屬軟玉類，玉料為摩氏礦石硬度6度。在還沒有金屬工具之前的新石器時代，至今尚沒有發現制作玉器的工具，先民們是如何開料、造型、磨研、雕琢、拋光、鑽孔的，一直是人們注意和關心的問題。一般認為是用解玉沙"如琢如磨"制成的。由於玉器質地堅硬，制作困難，每成一器，都十分費工費時。先民們制作成這樣的藝術品，手法古拙，形象傳神，實屬不易。它為研究先民們生產力發展水平和當時社會意識，提供了難得的實物資料。

Jade Carving Figure of a Head

The Neolithic Age（About 1000 years—4000 years ago）

H. 4.5cm.

Unearthed in 1976 at the site of Longshan Culture, Shen-mu County, Shaanxi.

This is a side of a head, formed by double side carving. On the top of its head, the hair was coiled as a lofty bun, round face, eagle-beak shaped nose, semi-opening mouth, the lower lips are longer, the cheek is bulging, according the material, the ears are the back, a line-carved eye on the back of the fore-heab-which occupies the half part. On the cheek, there is hole, under it is short and thin neck.

This like a middle-aded man's head, strong and honest. The outlines of the forehead, nose, mouth and ears are clear and eye carved in line in over-state location, which shows the beauty unified the abstraction and specific. Before 4900—4100 years, the ancestore espressed and fell about art, gave us full of fatasia. And this decoration shows the daybreak of the human civilization.

This jade belongs to the soft jade, which is the 6 of the Moer's hardness. At the Ne-olithic age without metal tools, up to now did not find the tools for making jade vessels, it is the problem how the ancestorrs to cut, from, carve, polish and making holes. Generally it was made by a kind of sand which polished the jade. Because of the hardness of the jade, it's very difficult of making jade vessels. it took a lot time of making one jade vessel. The ancestor made the art work like this, with simple and clumsy way, the shape is perfect, it's precious. It is the witness of researching the development of the productive forces and the society consciousness of that time.

玉雕人頭像
Jade Carving Figure of a Head

多面體煤精組印

西魏大統六年——十四年
（公元540年——548年）

通高4.5cm，寬4.35cm，重
75.7克

1981年於陝西旬陽縣城東
南出土

這件多面體印章，由煤精
刻制而成。它共有24個印面，由
16個正方形、8個三角形構成組
印。14個印面鐫有陰文魏體楷
書，分別為“臣信上章”、“臣信
上表”、“臣信上疏”、“臣信啟
事”、“大司馬印”、“大都督印”、
“刺史之印”、“柱國之印”、“獨
孤信白書”、“信白箋”、“信啟
事”及“耶敕”、全”、“密”。

印章的主人獨孤信，祖籍
雲中縣，鮮卑族。史載本名“如
原”，“美儀容，善騎射”。曾出任
過防城大都督，隴右十州大都
督、秦州刺史等職，官至西魏威
勢顯赫的“八柱國”之一。獨孤
信家族曾是中國歷史上顯赫一
時的家族，他的三個女兒分別
嫁給了北周明帝、隋文帝楊堅
和唐代開國皇帝李淵的父親。

此印集多印於一體，印文
為行文、上書、書信三種用途，
在我國現有出土文物中，確是
首次發現。

Polyhedron-jetted Seals

In the sixth years to 14th year of Datong of the Western Wei Dynasty（540 — 548 A. D.）

H. 4.5cm. W. 4.35cm. W. 75.7g.

Unearthed in 1981 at the south east of the Xunyang county，Shaanxi.

This polyhedron seal carved by black amber. It has 24 faces of seal，which combinated with 16 squares and 8 triangles. On 14 seal face carved with Wei Style regular script in intaglio，which are "Chen Xin Shang Zhang." "Chen Xin Shang Biao"."Chen Xin Shang Su.""Chen Xin Qi Shi"，"Da Si Ma Yin."， "Da Dudu Yin"，"Jia Shi Zhi Yin"."Zhu Guo Zhi Yin." "Du Gu Xin Bai Shu". "Xin Bai Jian". "Xin Qi Shi" and "Ye Chi" "Quan"，"Mi".

The master of this group of seals was DuGu xin，his ancestral home was at Yun Zhong County，he was Sienpi. Historical recorded his name was "Ru Yuan"，Handsome face and good at shooting. "he was gained a lot of officals such as "Fang Cheng Da Dudu". Long You shi zhou Da dudu，etc. Dugu xin's family was a great family in illustrious honour，his three daughters were marriaged with the Emperor Ming of Northeren Zhou Dynasty and Emperor Wen of Sui Dynasty and the first emperor Li Yuan's father of the Tang Dynasty.

This is a special seasl with scription，letterrs several way，which is the first time of unearthed rilics.

多面體煤精組印
Polyhedron—jetted Seals

伏虎圓雕羅漢

北宋（公元960—1127年）

通高38cm

1980年于陝西富縣柏山寺塔第三層龕洞內發現

羅漢光頭，長臉豐頤，高鼻闊嘴，雙耳下垂，身披雙領袈裟，結跏趺座。左側蹲立雛犰。羅漢坐在方形座上，雙目微閉，雙唇緊合，寧神靜默，含蓄溫雅。

據專家考證，此尊羅漢是十八羅漢中的第六羅漢跋陀羅，他大智大勇，具有超凡法力。

圓雕以形傳神，形神兼備，刀法洗練，刻劃精微。它抓取人物最富感情特征的瞬間，面部刻劃細膩，維妙維肖，衣褶概括大方，灑脫得體，使鮮活的生命和流動的情感洋溢其中，有極強的整體感和呼之欲出的感染力。圓雕把羅漢的泰然自若和猛獸的馴順恭良表現得恰到好處，襯托出羅漢的聰慧睿智，不同凡響，是難得的古代雕刻藝術珍品。

Figure of Arhat Subding Tiger

Northern Song Dynasty (960—1127 A. D.)

H. 38cm.

Unearthed in 1980 from the tower of Banshan Temple, Fuxian County, Shaanxi.

This Arhat is bareheared, long face is plentiful, with high nose and wide mouth, two ears are dangling, wearing a double-collar Kasaya which tying covered the base. On his left, squatting a young tiger. the arhat is sitting on the base, closing his eyes and lips, keeping silence, who is embody and gentle.

Texual researched by the experts, this arhat is the sixth arhat named batuoluo, who is wisdom and brave and has superb magical power.

This figure is graceful and vigourous, the method of carving is perfect and fine. The creator caught the feature of this arhat, facial expression is fine and vivid, the folds of the cloth is free and easy, which shows the activity life and flowing feeling are filled in them, full of fantasia and power of artistic. The figure expressed the calmness of the arhat and the gentleness of the tiger in a perfect way, reflects the arhat wisdom and unique style, it is rare precious sculture gem.

伏虎圓雕羅漢
Figure of Arhat Subding Tiger

幻方鐵板

元代（公元1271年—1368年）

長 14cm，寬 14cm

1957年於陝西西安市元代安西王府遺址出土

幻方鐵板上每行均由六個數字排列，組成方陣，不論縱行或橫行，或對角線上的數字，相加之和都是111。這個蘊含着數學原理的六六幻方，在古代被視為奇妙的神秘之物。人們把它鄭重地裝進石函，埋入房基中，用作鎮宅和防災避邪的吉祥物。

幻方上共有36個古代阿拉伯人使用的數字。原來，阿拉伯人一直使用28個字田作為記數符號，歐州人則一直用羅馬數字記數。早在公元4世紀以前，古印度人已經首創了包括"0"在內的十個數字符號。直到公元8世紀，叙利亞的阿拉伯人發現了印度數字的優點，幷在其帝國中推廣，后又通過西班牙傳入歐洲，逐漸取代了羅馬數字，幷傳播到世界各地。鐵板上的數字實際是真正的阿拉伯數字，現在被稱為阿拉伯數字的0，1，2，3，4，5，6，7，8，9則是印度數字，是古代印度人對世界文化寶庫最偉大的貢獻。幻方鐵板是我國數學上應用阿拉伯數字最早的實物記錄。

幻方鐵板的出土地點在今天西安火車站東北三公里處，是元代安西王府的遺址。安西王府是忽必烈的三兒子忙哥刺的王宮。著名的意大利旅行家馬可·波羅在游記中曾記述說，他曾親歷府上，這里宏偉王宮高牆環繞，方圓八公里，"構造整齊勻稱，堂皇華麗的程度，簡直無以復加。宮中有許多大理石砌成的殿堂和樓閣，裝飾着圖畫、金箔幷配上最美的天藍色。"幻方鐵板就埋在這座王宮的基礎中，它也為研究元代宗教和習俗提供了實物資料。

幻方鐵板數字：

28	4	3	31	35	10
36	18	21	24	11	1
7	23	12	17	22	30
8	13	26	19	16	29
5	20	15	14	25	32
27	33	34	6	2	9

Magical Square Iron Board

Yuan Dynasty（1271 — 1368 A. D.）

L. 14cm W. 14cm.

Unearthed in 1957 from the king's residence of the Yuan Dynasty, Xian City, Shaanxi.

Each line on the hoard formed with six numbers, and forming a square formation, no matter the line or vertical line and the opposite angle, the plus of these numbers on them usally are 111. This magical square with maths principke, which was regarded as a fatancy and mysterious matter. The people huried it into a stone hox and into the foundation of the room, put it as the lucky matter of guarding residence and getting rid of the phosts.

There are 36 numbers of Ancient Arabian on the board Originally, the Arabian used 28 numbers as the symbol of counting, the European used the Roman numbers. And before four century A. D., the Ancient Indian created the ten numbers. Including zero. Up to 8 century, the Arabian of Syria found the advantages of indian numbers, andspread in the Empire, later propagated into Europe by Spian, and istead of the the Roman number on the iron board are the real Arabian munbers, a numbers, and nowadays-called Arabian numbers 0, 1, 2, 3, 4, 5, 6, 7, 8, 9, are the Indian numbers, which is the great contribution of the Ancient Indian for the World Cultural treasure-house. And the magical board is the record about the using of Arabian numbers in Chinese Maths.

The place where unearthed the magical board is at the 3km location of the northeast of the Xian Railway station, where is the size of the King Anxi of the Yuan Dynasty. The residence of King Anxi was the Palace of the third son Mang glela of Huhilie. The famous Italian traveller Marc Polo wrote in his journey like this, he came into the residence of King Anxi, here with great splendid palaces and has the ciucumference of 8 km, and the book had the inscription means the palace was splendid and magnificent. This magical iron hoard is hurried in the foundation of this King's Residence, which is the witness of researching the religion and the custom of the Yuan Dynasty.

幻方鐵板
Magical Square Iron Board

中國歷史年代簡表

夏	約公元前21世紀──前16世紀
商	約公元前16世紀──前11世紀
西周	約公元前1066年──前771年
東周	公元前770年──前256年
春秋時代	公元前770年──前476年
戰國時代	公元前475年──前221年
秦	公元前221年──前206年
西漢	公元前206年──前8年
東漢	公元25年──220年
三國魏	公元220年──265年
蜀	公元221年──263年
吳	公元222年──280年
西晉	公元265年──316年
東晉	公元317年──420年
十六國	公元304年──公元439年
南朝	公元420年──589年
北朝	公元386年──581年
隋	公元581年──618年
唐	公元618年──907年
五代十國	公元907年──979年
北宋	公元960年──1127年
南宋	公元1127年──1279年
遼	公元916年──1125年
西夏	公元1032年──1227年
金	公元1115年──1234年
元	公元1271年──1368年
明	公元1368年──1644年
清	公元1644年──1911年

THE ANNALS DYNASTIES

XIA   21th centuary B. C. —16th centuary B. C.

Shang   16th centuary B. C. —1066 B. C.

Western Zhou   1066 B. C. —771 B. C.

Eastern Zhou   770 B. C. —256 B. C.

Spring and Autumn Period   770 B. C. — 476 B. C.

Warring State Period   476 B. C. —221 B. C.

Qin   221 B. C. —206 B. C.

Western Han   206 B. C. —8 A. D.

Eastern Han   25—220 A. D.

Three Kindoms

Wei   220—265 A. D.

Shu · 221—263 A. D.

Wu   222—280 A. D.

Western Jin   265—316 A. D.

Eastern Jin   317—420 A. D.

Sixteen Kindoms   304—439 A. D.

Southern Dynasty   420—589 A. D.

Northern Dynasty   386—581 A. D.

Sui   581—618 A. D.

Tang   618—907 A. D.

Five Dynasties and ten kindoms   907—979 A. D.

Northern Song   960—1127 A. D.

Southern Song   1127—1279 A. D.

Liao   916—1125 A. D.

Western Xia   1032—1227 A. D.

Jin   1115—1234 A. D.

Yuan   1271—1368 A. D.

Ming   1368—1644 A. D.

Qing   1644—1911 A. D.

審　　訂: 陳緒萬

攝　　影: 邱子渝

英文翻譯: 明　哲

責任編輯: 于永錦　徐未未

裝幀設計: 徐未未　曹金娥

封面設計: 梁京京　李　禮

責任校對: 張　星

督 印 人: 梁京京

陝西歷史博物館
館藏精品鑒賞

楊培鈞　著

陝西人民教育出版社

新華書店經銷

深圳時代設計印務有限公司印刷

(0755-2244640　2244645　2271779)

889× 1194 毫米　16 開本　12 印張

1996 年 1 月第 1 版　1996 年 1 月第 1 次印刷

印數: 1-3000

ISBN7-5419-6331-3 / K・28 (0013800)